ADVENTURES
IN ENGLISH
Experiences in Language

The Laidlaw Language Experiences Program

LISTENING AND TALKING *Experiences in Language*

LISTENING, READING, AND TALKING *Experiences in Language*

LISTENING, READING, TALKING, AND WRITING
Experiences in Language

ADVENTURES IN ENGLISH *Experiences in Language*

EXPLORING IN ENGLISH *Experiences in Language*

DISCOVERY IN ENGLISH *Experiences in Language*

PROGRESS IN ENGLISH *Experiences in Language*

GROWTH IN ENGLISH *Experiences in Language*

POWER IN ENGLISH *Experiences in Language*

SUCCESS IN ENGLISH *Experiences in Language*

ADVENTURES
IN ENGLISH
Experiences in Language

John S. Hand
Director
Indiana Facilitator Center
Logansport Community School Corporation
Logansport, Indiana

Dr. Wayne Harsh
Associate Professor
Department of English
University of California-Davis
Davis, California

Dr. James W. Ney
Professor of English
Arizona State University
Tempe, Arizona

Dr. Harold G. Shane
University Professor of Education
School of Education
Indiana University
Bloomington, Indiana

LAIDLAW BROTHERS · PUBLISHERS
A Division of Doubleday & Company, Inc.

RIVER FOREST, ILLINOIS

Palo Alto, California   Atlanta, Georgia   Dallas, Texas
New York, New York   Toronto, Canada

Cover design by Donald C. Meighan

Chapter-opening abstracts by Donald C. Meighan

> Both reality and abstraction, language is an organic whole made up of complex and intricately related parts. The chapter-opening abstracts suggest its patterns, its symmetries, and its colors.

Woodcuts by Corinne and Robert Borja

Other contributing artists:

Dev Appleyard	Stan Ekman	Art Lutz
Auto-Write, Division of Boecher Studio	Jack Haesly	Donald C. Meighan
	Paul Hazelrigg	Edward Ostendorf
James Buckley	William Heckler	John Walter
Francis Chase	Robert Johnson	Marilou Wise
Ralph Creasman	Sid Jordan	
Tom Dunnington	Janet LaSalle	

ACKNOWLEDGMENTS

"Galoshes" from the book STORIES TO BEGIN ON by Rhoda W. Bacmeister: Copyright 1940 by E. P. Dutton & Co., Inc. Renewal © 1968 by Rhoda W. Bacmeister. Published by E. P. Dutton & Co., Inc. and reprinted with their permission. / "One, Two, Three" by Henry Cuyler Bunner: From POEMS by Henry Cuyler Bunner (Charles Scribner's Sons, 1884). / "Tardiness" by Gelett Burgess: Reprinted from GOOPS AND HOW TO BE THEM by Gelett Burgess, published by J. B. Lippincott Company. Copyright, 1900, 1928 by Gelett Burgess. / "Some Cook" by John Ciardi: Reprinted from THE MAN WHO SANG THE SILLIES by John Ciardi. © 1961 by The Curtis Publishing Company. / "The Reason for the Pelican" by John Ciardi: Copyright, ©, 1955 by The Curtis Publishing Company. From the book THE REASON FOR THE PELICAN by John Ciardi: Copyright, ©, 1959 by John Ciardi. Reprinted by permission of J. B. Lippincott Company. / "This Man Came from Nowhere" from I MET A MAN by John Ciardi: Published, 1961, by Houghton Mifflin Company, and reprinted with their permission. / "Twenty Froggies" by George Cooper: Reprinted from A CHILD'S BOOK OF POEMS, published, 1969, by Grosset & Dunlap, Inc. Pictures by Gyo Fujikawa. / "The Kayak" reprinted from A CHILD'S BOOK OF POEMS, published, 1969, by Grosset & Dunlap, Inc. Pictures by Gyo Fujikawa. / "Two Geese" by Daniel Hooley from *Meeting Music: Music for Young Americans,* Second Edition, by Richard C. Berg, Lee Kjelson, and Eugene W. Troth: Published, 1966, by American Book Company, and reprinted with their

(ACKNOWLEDGMENTS continued on page 336.)

ISBN 0-8445-2423-9

Copyright © 1975 by Laidlaw Brothers, Publishers

A Division of Doubleday & Company, Inc.

Printed in the United States of America

8 9 10 11 12 13 14 15   3 2 1 0 9 8

CONTENTS

9

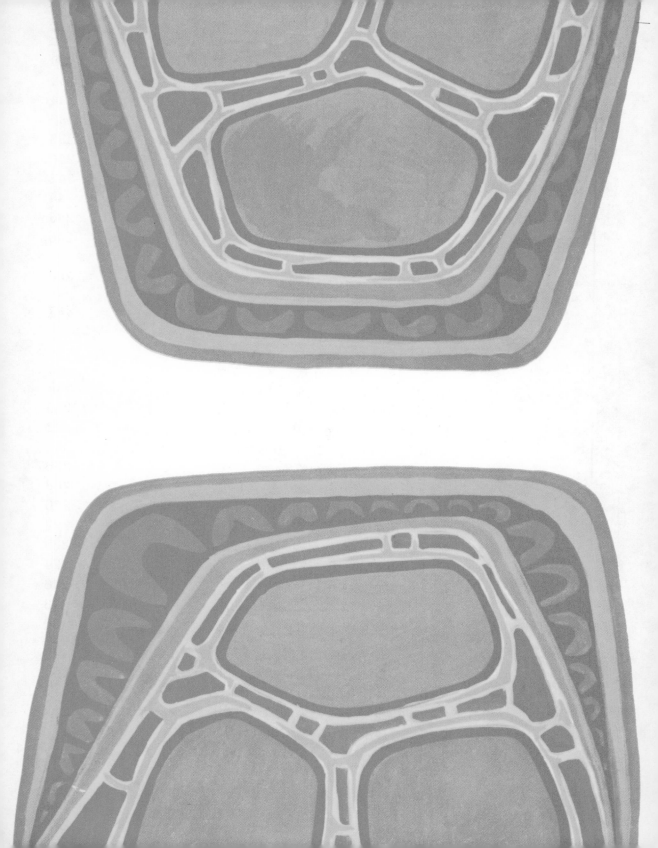

1. Last Names

The man shown in the picture softens iron by heating it. Then he can pound it into the shape he wants. This man is a blacksmith.

Long ago, many villages had a blacksmith. People called him the smith.

At that time, many English people had only a first name. This sometimes caused problems. In some villages more than one person had the same name. One way to solve the problems was to give each person a last name. Would Smith have been a good last name for a blacksmith? Why?

For Discussion

A. What may have been the special meaning of each last name below when it was first used?

1. Longfellow   3. Doolittle   5. Drinkwater
2. Short   4. Scattergood   6. Makepeace

B. Here are some more last names made up long ago. What special meaning might each name have had?

1. Fishman   3. Baker   5. Lake
2. Miner   4. Knight   6. Field

C. What would have been a good last name for each person described below?

1. Someone who was a shoemaker
2. Someone who was a cook
3. Someone who made bells
4. Someone who lived on a cliff
5. Someone who earned money by singing

D. Which of the last names of people in your class seem to have a special meaning? What do you think the meaning was when the name was first used?

ON YOUR OWN

Collect some last names that seem to have a meaning. Draw a picture showing what one of the names means. Show your collection of names and your picture to the class.

Cook

2. Sounds and Language

The poem below gives the words of a song. Read the poem. Then answer the questions about it.

TWO GEESE

Two geese sat in the yellow straw,
Sat and hissed at all they saw;
A boy came by and said: "Hi, hi!"
To the geese that sat on the yellow straw;
Hi there, geese!
Ssss! Ssss!
Hi there, geese!
Ssss! Ssss!
Hi there, geese!
Ssss! Ssss!
Hi there, geese!
Ssss! Ssss!
Such silly geese I never saw!
I don't want your yellow straw.

—Daniel Hooley

14

- What sounds did the geese make?

- What meaning were the two geese trying to express?

Think about the way the boy used sounds to express his meaning.

- What words did he use?

- What meaning was the boy trying to express?

Think again about the sounds the geese made. These sounds did not make words. They did not make sentences.

Now think about the sounds the boy used. His sounds made words and sentences. The sounds were speech sounds.

The boy was using language. The geese were not. All languages are spoken by putting together speech sounds to make words and sentences.

For Discussion

A. Can any animals speak language? How do you know?

B. What sounds that are not words or sentences could you use to express these meanings?

1. That you have a hurt finger
2. That something is funny
3. That you agree with something you hear
4. That you don't believe something you hear
5. That you hate the taste of burned toast

3. Word Order in Sentences

Read the group of words in the picture. Do the words make a sentence?

Now read the words in each group below.

1. Goldfish Peter the fed.

2. Fed goldfish Peter the.

3. Peter fed the goldfish.

- Which words do you see in each group?

- Which group sounds like a sentence?

Look at this group of words. Does this group sound like a sentence?

    food   ate   goldfish   the   the

The words above can be arranged in many different ways. What are some of the ways? Which of the ways would you use to make a sentence? Why?

Tell what to do to make sentences out of these groups of words.

1. Helen   puppy   has   a
2. my   I   coat   tore
3. us   Donald   was   for   waiting

For Practice

For More Practice
See Page 317

Oral Put each group of words below in sentence order.

1. Ellen a wanted doll
2. had she no money buy it to
3. came birthday her
4. father gave doll her Ellen a
5. a flew plane by
6. very close was it
7. saw letters on its we tail
8. was gone soon it
9. good-bye waved we

Written Use each group of words to make a sentence.

1. delicious tastes pie this
2. going we fishing are
3. don't I Susan know
4. caught butterfly Carol a
5. the Raymond drank juice
6. time it's leave to
7. Barbara chicken does like not
8. its cat the hurt paw
9. pony I a have named Sandy

ON YOUR OWN

Find a long sentence that you can read. Write the sentence on a strip of paper like this.

George Washington was the father of his country.

Cut the sentence into separate words. Then give the words to a friend. Ask him to put the words back into sentence order.

17

4. Changing the Meaning

Would you say that both sentences below are true?

Angela called Alberto.
Alberto called Angela.

Look at both sentences above. Then answer these questions.

- What words are the same?

- Are the words in the same order in both sentences?

- Do both sentences mean the same thing?

Both sentences have the same words but different meanings. Why? Is the order of words in a sentence important to meaning?

For Discussion

A. What are two things that give meaning to an English sentence?

B. What would you have to do to make two sentences from each group of words below?

1. beagle   the   Melissa   chased

2. ball   hit   the   Eric

3. invited   Greta   Frieda   to her party

Oral A. Make a sentence from each group of words below. Then make another sentence from each group of words by changing the word order.

1. Joyce new liked girl the
2. told June a Gloria secret
3. the the dog cat chased

B. Read the sentences below. Make four other sentences by changing the word order in the sentences.

1. Ted invited Bill to a party.
2. Ted took Bill to a horse farm.
3. The boys saw the horses.
4. The horses raced the boys to the stable.

Written For each sentence below, write a new sentence using the same words in a different order.

1. The monkey saw the snake.
2. The roofers came before the bricklayers.
3. Lynn walked with Denise.
4. Gerald gave his mother a gift.
5. The sea is as blue as the sky.
6. Patrick threw the ball to Louis.
7. The rat looked at the cat.
8. A lion is bigger than a tiger.
9. Stefanie gave Mary a ride.
10. Peter runs faster than Dexter.

ON YOUR OWN

Match the sentences and pictures.

The dog bit the man.

The man bit the dog.

Make up sentences that are funny when you change the order of the words. Draw a picture for each sentence. Give your sentences to a friend. Ask him to change the order of the words. Ask him to make pictures for the new sentences.

19

5. Writing Names

Read each sentence. Then answer these questions. How do you know you are right?

- What girls are named?

- What boy is named?

- What pet is named?

Give a pearl to Pearl.
Please give a penny to Penny.
Tom Wren saw a wren.
Look at the spot on Spot.

Think about your answers to the questions above. What kind of letter begins each part of a person's name? What kind of letter begins a pet's name?

For Discussion

Which words in italics below would you begin with capital letters? Why?

1. Give my friend *rose* a *rose*.
2. I called my *turtle, turtle*.
3. Edward *bell* rang the church *bell*.
4. My kitten feels *silky*. I named her *silky*.

For Practice

Written Write these sentences. Use capital letters where they belong.

1. My name is leroy.
2. I have a new puppy.
3. I named it ginger.
4. Two girls, teresa and vanessa, came to see ginger.

For More Practice
See Page 317

5. Ginger ran under the porch.
6. When ginger tried to come out again, she got stuck.
7. My little brother, michael, squeezed under the porch.
8. He got ginger out for teresa and vanessa to see.

20

6. Writing *Mr.*, *Mrs.*, and *Miss*

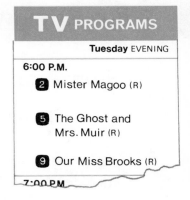

Read the names of the programs. In which is the leading part played by a woman? By a man?

When written as part of a person's name, *Mister*, *Mr.*, *Mrs.*, and *Miss* are called **titles.**

Look at the titles in these names. Answer the questions.

Mr. Rosen   Mrs. Rosen   Miss Rosen

■ What kind of letter begins each title?

■ Which titles end with a period?

For Discussion

A. In which sentence below is *Miss* used as a title? How do you know?

1. She is Miss Susan Shaw.   **2.** She is a lovely miss.

B. Why is a period used after *Mr.* and not after *Mister* when they are titles?

For Practice

For More Practice
See Page 318

Written   A. Write these names. Use *Mr.* as a title for each man. Use *Mrs.* as a title for each woman.

1. Peter Bellucci
2. Nancy Hurst
3. Anne Lehman
4. Ronald Pozen

B. Write these names. Use *Mr.* as a title for each man. Use *Miss* as a title for each woman.

1. Maria Territo
2. Anthony York
3. Mary Zajic
4. Patrick Reilly

21

7. For Review

Read and discuss the questions below.

A. The kitten, the boy, and the girl are all using sounds. Which one is using language? How did you decide?

B. Which group of words below is in the right order to make a sentence? How do you know?

1. a picture painted Carlos
2. picture painted a Carlos
3. Carlos painted a picture
4. Carlos picture a painted

C. How can you change the meaning of each sentence below without changing the words in it? What sentences can you make?

1. Robert chased Bruce.
2. Irene likes the kitten.
3. Kurt saw his teacher.
4. Carl gave a gift to Tom.

D. Which letters in these names would you capitalize if you were writing them? Why? Where would you use periods? Why?

1. michael sullivan
2. mrs david hardy

3. miss jane nemec
4. mr george hogan

Read the directions for each exercise below. Follow the directions, writing your answers on your own paper.

A. Decide how to put each group of words below into sentence order. Then write each sentence.

1. letter   a   wrote   Frank
2. a   quarter   found   Alan
3. jacket   my   lost   I
4. candy   like   I   that

B. Change the meaning of each sentence below by changing the order of the words in it. Write each new sentence.

5. Roberta wrote a letter to Bernice.
6. Mark liked the puppy.
7. Frances bought some flowers for her mother.
8. Angela went to a party for Arlene.

C. Decide where you would use capital letters and periods in these names. Then write the names.

9. miss ann cox
10. mr alan dodge
11. mrs david marx
12. bruce ford

23

9. Talking about Families

Each picture on these two pages shows a family that lives in a different part of the world. Look at the pictures. Answer the questions below.

- Besides a mother, what members does each family have?

- What are the families doing together?

- What kinds of things might each family member do to help the other members?

Dinner Time in Africa

Monkmeyer Press

'Zentrale Farbbild Agentur

Play Time in Australia

24

Make believe that you can visit all three families in the pictures. Then answer these questions.

1. Could you help each family at mealtime? How?
2. Could you help with the family chores? What could you do to help?

Activities

Form groups with four or five children in each group. Then do these things.

1. Form a make-believe family. Choose children to be the mother, the father, and each child.
2. Draw a picture of yourself doing something to help the others in your make-believe family. For example, if you are the mother, you can show yourself sewing on buttons.
3. Put all the pictures on a long strip of paper. Tell the class what the members of your make-believe family do. Use the pictures to help you think of what to say.

Birthday Time in Asia

25

Monkmeyer Press

10. Acting Out Stories by Yourself

Read the poem. What story does the poem tell?

SOME COOK!

Johnny made a custard
In the pepper pot.
Flavored it with mustard,
Put in quite a lot
Of garlic fried in olive oil,
Brought the custard to a boil,
Ate it up and burned his tongue—

You shouldn't cook when you're too young.

—JOHN CIARDI

Read the poem again. Think of a way to act out its story, using only your hands and face.

■ How could you use your hands to show how the custard was made?

■ How could you use your face to show how the custard tasted?

For Discussion

A. Which of the things shown in the pictures have you done at home?

B. What story does each picture make you think of? What parts of the story could you tell with your hands? With your face?

Activities

A. By yourself, do these things.

1. Think of some problem that you had when you were by yourself in your family. Perhaps you were doing something with clothes or with food. Perhaps you were helping with chores.

2. Make a picture to show what you were doing that caused the problem.

B. Form groups with four or five children in each group. Bring your picture to the group but do not show it yet. Use your body and face to act out the story your picture tells. The others may try to guess the story. After the guesses are made, show your picture.

11. Acting Out a Story with Others

Read the following poem softly to yourself. The poet made up the word *norful*. What does his made-up word mean?

TARDINESS

Goodness gracious sakes alive!
Mother said, "Come home at five!"
Now the clock is striking six,
I am in a norful fix!
She will think I can't be trusted,
And she'll say that she's disgusted!

—GELETT BURGESS

Read the poem again. Answer these questions about the person who is speaking.

- Did he plan to be late?

- How did he feel about being late?

- Did his mother expect him to be late?

- What might she say when he comes in?

Your class might want to make a play out of this poem. The play should have two scenes. The first scene could be in a friend's house. Where could the second scene be?

Talk about what your class could do to put on a play about being late. Answer these questions.

1. Where can the play be given? What characters are needed for each scene?

2. How might the tardy child act when he hears the clock strike six? What might he say to his friend? What might his friend say?

3. How might the tardy child act when he sees his mother? What might he say?

4. How might the mother act when she sees her child? What might she say?

Activities

Form groups of four or five children each. Each group can put on a play.

Here are some suggestions.

1. Before you begin acting, make two clocks for use in the play. You can use the clocks to help show a change of scene.

2. Act out each scene two or three times, using the clocks to help show a change of scene. Each child may take a different part each time. Each time you give the play, talk about how to make it better.

29

12. Making Animal Stories to Act Out

In some stories the author uses animal characters that talk. The story below is like this. Both characters are blue jays.

MOTHER JAY: Jasper, you're the oldest one in the family. You should help do the work.

JASPER JAY: I'll help. What can I do?

MOTHER JAY: Well, you can clean your room. That'll help us all.

JASPER JAY: Where can I begin?

MOTHER JAY: For one thing, throw out that string of beads.

JASPER JAY: Oh, Mother. Uncle Albert gave me those beads. I just have to keep them. Isn't there something else I can throw out?

MOTHER JAY: How about that red ribbon?

How do you think Jasper will answer his mother? What might she say then? How might the story end?

Suppose that your class wanted to make up an animal story for two persons to act out. One person could play the mother or father. The other could play the part of a young animal. Answering these questions may help you think of stories.

1. What could a mother beaver say to a baby beaver who was afraid to cut down trees? What could the baby beaver say? How might the story end?

2. What could a father possum say to a baby possum who didn't want to learn to climb trees? What could the baby possum say? How might the story end?

3. What could a mother duck say to a baby duck who didn't want to learn to swim? What could the baby duck say? How might the story end?

Activities

Form groups of four or five children. Each group may choose an animal story to act out. Choose a story from those you worked with in this lesson.

1. Make something for the animals to wear. For example, the blue jays might wear a headband that has blue feathers.

2. Take turns acting out your play. Talk about ways to make it better.

13. Listening to Poetry

Listen as your teacher reads the following poem to you.

ADVICE TO CHILDREN

For a domestic, gentle pet,
A hippopotamus I'd get—
     They're very kind and mild.
I'm sure if you but purchase one
You'll find 'twill make a lot of fun
     For any little child.

Select one of a medium size,
With glossy fur and soft blue eyes,
     Then brush and comb him well.
With wreaths of flowers his forehead deck,
And from a ribbon round his neck
     Suspend a silver bell.

If it should be a rainy day,
Up in the nursery he will play
     With Baby, Tot and Ted;
Upon the rocking-horse he'll ride,
Or merrily he'll run and hide
     Beneath a chair or bed.

And when he wants to take a nap,
He'll cuddle up in Totty's lap,
    As quiet as a mouse.
Just try it, and you'll soon agree
A hippopotamus should be
    A pet in every house.

          —CAROLYN WELLS

Listen as your teacher reads the poem again. Be ready to answer these questions.

- What advice does the poet give?
- Could anyone take the advice? Why or why not?

For Discussion

Read aloud the parts of the poem which answer the following questions.

1. What things make a hippopotamus a good pet?
2. What can children do to have fun with a pet hippopotamus?
3. What can the hippopotamus do to have fun?

Activities

A. Draw a picture of a hippopotamus. Make him look as though he likes being a pet.

B. Show your picture in class. Tell what a hippopotamus might like about being your family pet.

33

CHAPTER 2

1. Making Up Last Names

The man shown in the picture lived in Turkey long ago. His friends gave him the name *Us*. In their language *Us* meant "man with a long mustache." Was *Us* a good name for the man? Why?

The boy shown in the picture is the son of *Us*. When the boy grew up, he needed a last name. People named him after his father. They did this by adding *enko*, meaning "son of," to *Us*.

Us **+** enko → Usenko

The name *Usenko* means "son of a man with a long mustache." Was this a good last name for the son? Why?

People who spoke other languages were sometimes named after their fathers, too. The statements below show how this was done. The part in color means *son of*.

Jack **+ son** → Jackson

Peter **+ sen** → Petersen

Len **+ in** → Lenin

Mac + Donald → MacDonald

Mc + Clure → McClure

The name *Jackson* means "son of Jack." What does each of the other names mean?

For Discussion

What last name can you make up by completing each statement below? What does each last name mean?

1. Bob **+** enko
2. Zim **+** in
3. Bil **+** enko
4. Jacob **+** sen

5. John **+** son
6. Mac **+** Arthur
7. Mc **+** Amis
8. Mac **+** Neil

ON YOUR OWN

Make a list of last names that have a word part meaning "son of." Show your list to some friends. See if they know any other last names that you can add to your list.

2. Speech Sounds in Words

The word that names the first picture has three speech sounds in it. Read the other two words. Listen to see how many speech sounds they have.

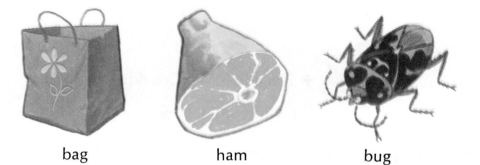

bag   ham   bug

- Which word has the same beginning sound as *bag?*

- Which word has the same middle sound as *ham?*

- Which word has the same last sound as *bug?*

Now change the first sound in *bag.* Use the beginning sound you hear in *rim.* Which of these words did you make?

tab   rag   nag

Next, change the middle sound in *bug.* Use the middle sound you hear in *ran.* Which of these words did you make?

beg   bag   big

Change the third sound in *ham.* Use the third sound you hear in *cat.* Which of these words did you make?

         hag   hat   half

A. What word would you use to name each picture below? How many speech sounds are in each word?

1. bed   **2.** man   **3.** rug

B. Which sound must you change in *bed* to make *bud*?

C. Which sound must you change in *man* to make *mad*?

D. Which sound must you change in *rug* to make *hug*?

For Practice

Oral   A. Make six other words by changing the beginning sound of each word below.

1. tan   **4.** lad
2. bib   **5.** peg
3. dot   **6.** cup

B. Make other words by changing the middle sound of each word in the next group.

1. lad   **4.** rug
2. not   **5.** big
3. hem   **6.** sat

C. Make other words by changing the last sound of each word below.

1. fat   **4.** sack
2. him   **5.** lad
3. men   **6.** calf

39

3. Letters for Sounds

The larger girl has a cap in her hands. What does the smaller girl have in hers?

Listen for the number of speech sounds as you say each word below to yourself.

cap   cape

- ■ How many speech sounds do you hear in each word?

- ■ How many letters are needed to write each word?

The words below have the same middle sound as *cape*. How is this sound spelled in each word?

paid   break

Which of the following words
have one letter for each sound?

1. seal	**5.** bowl
2. lad	**6.** bear
3. puff	**7.** lake
4. hill	**8.** man

**For
Practice**

Oral A. Find the two words in each row that have just one letter for each sound.

1. tag	tell	tan
2. sniff	if	Tim
3. pat	bag	coal
4. till	pig	mist
5. mat	meal	pan

B. Find the two words in each row that have two letters for the sound at the end.

1. putt	puff	but
2. will	moon	muff
3. rod	odd	hill
4. bell	less	cool
5. peg	egg	mill

C. Find the words in each row that have the same sound but different spellings for this sound.

1. seal	peel	net
2. tape	buy	lie
3. poke	hot	bowl
4. bear	bare	bad
5. pool	mud	rule

41

4. Statements

Read this poem just for fun.

THE LITTLE TURTLE

There was a little turtle.
He lived in a box.
He swam in a puddle.
He climbed on the rocks.

He snapped at a mosquito.
He snapped at a flea.
He snapped at a minnow.
And he snapped at me.

He caught the mosquito.
He caught the flea.
He caught the minnow.
But he didn't catch me.

—Vachel Lindsay

Read the poem to yourself, sentence by sentence. See whether or not each sentence tells you something.

Sentences that tell you something are called **statements.** What mark is used at the end of a statement?

For Discussion

Which of the sentences below are statements? How do you know?

1. A pear is good.   **3.** My father is a bricklayer.

2. The bus is here.   **4.** Is the apple good?

Oral Add a word to each example below to make it a statement.

1. Pears are very —.
2. The boys were very —.
3. — is here.
4. — was here.
5. The girl was —.
6. Mr. Clark is a —.
7. The man was a —.
8. — fly.
9. Sirens —.
10. John sold his —.

ON YOUR OWN

Write three sentences about each of the make-believe animals. Each sentence should tell something different about the animals. Ask someone to read your sentences to see if they are statements.

43

5. One Kind of Question

The two girls, Sue and Ann, are playing a guessing game. To begin, Ann says, "I am thinking of something. Try to tell its name."

The game goes on like this.

SUE: Is it near me?
ANN: Yes.
SUE: Is it yellow?
ANN: No.
SUE: Is it a cookie?
ANN: Yes.

Sentences that need an answer are called **questions**. Some questions need a *yes* or *no* answer. This kind of question is called a **yes/no question**.

Now study the following words and sentences. Which of the words on the cards are used in the sentences below them?

It is near me.   Is it near me?

- Are the same words used in both sentences?

- What words have changed order in the second sentence?

- What mark is used at the end of the question?

44

A. Read sentences *a* and *b* below. Answer the questions.

> **a.** It is yellow.
>
> **b.** Is it yellow?

1. Is sentence *a* a statement? How can you tell?

2. Is sentence *b* a *yes/no* question? How can you tell?

B. What would you do to the order of the words in the sentences below to make them into *yes/no* questions?

1. It is purple.

2. The trucks are rolling again.

3. The air hammers were pounding.

For Practice

For More Practice
See Page 318

Oral A. Change each statement below into a *yes/no* question.

1. The melon is very ripe.
2. Apples are cheap this year.
3. The boys were in the street.
4. My friend was hurt yesterday.
5. The pencil is in my pocket.

B. Change each *yes/no* question below into a statement.

1. Is your jacket new?
2. Are your hands clean?
3. Is the girl here?
4. Were the boys there?
5. Is your father a craftsman?

ON YOUR OWN

You and a friend may enjoy the game that Sue and Ann played. Begin each question with *is, are, was, were,* or *am.* Take turns making up questions.

45

6. Yes/No Questions with *Do* and *Did*

Read the sentences in the box below. Which sentence is a statement? What do you call the other sentence?

The boys dig holes.

Do the boys dig holes?

Read the above sentences again. Answer these questions.

- What words are the same in both sentences?

- What word do you find in the question that is not in the statement?

Now read the statement and question in the box below.

- What words are the same in both sentences?

- What change was made in the word *dug?*

- What word do you find in the question that is not in the statement?

The boys dug holes.

Did the boys dig holes?

Look at the examples in both boxes again. What two words can you add to some statements to change them to questions?

For Discussion

What would you do to make *yes/no* questions from these statements by adding *do* or *did?*

1. Boys like to ride bicycles.
2. They sometimes ride on a busy street.
3. A boy fell from his bicycle yesterday.
4. He fell in front of a truck.
5. The driver hit the brakes.
6. The truck swerved and skidded.
7. The truck missed the boy.

For Practice

Oral A. Change each statement to a *yes/no* question beginning with *do.*

1. Children play here.
2. The boys need shoes.
3. The nurses need jobs.
4. The fighters seem old.
5. You like to play.
6. Butterflies have colorful wings.

B. What statement can you make from each *yes/no* question by taking a word out of each question?

1. Do geese honk?
2. Do you see the truck?

For More Practice
See Page 319

3. Do rockets move swiftly?
4. Do cameras tell the truth?
5. Do you like music?
6. Do fish swim fast?

C. What statement can you make from each *yes/no* question?

1. Did the man buy gas?
2. Did the man give you stamps?
3. Did the rain seem cold?
4. Did the mice run?
5. Did the street get rough?
6. Did the snow melt?

47

7. Names of Streets and Schools

Read each sentence below. Look at the words in color. In what way are these words alike? How are they different?

There are *oak* trees along *Oak* Street.
There are *elm* trees along *Elm* Avenue.
The school near a *park* is called *Park* Avenue School.

■ Which words are used to name each street, avenue, and school?

■ What kind of letter is used to begin each word in the names?

For Discussion

Which of the words in italics in each sentence would you begin with a capital letter? Why?

1. He bought *apples* on *apple lane*.
2. The *main* road follows *main street*.
3. Our *school* is called *potter school*.

For More Practice
See Page 319

For Practice

Written Write the name of each street or school below. Use capital letters where they belong.

1. holly avenue
2. st. charles street
3. church street
4. poplar avenue
5. harwood lane
6. first avenue school
7. jay school
8. clearmont school
9. central high school

48

8. Names of Cities and States

Read these sentences. What cities and states are named? What kind of letter is used to begin the name of a city and the name of a state?

Boston is a city in the state of Massachusetts.
Santa Fe is a city in New Mexico.
Los Angeles is a city in California.

For Discussion

Which words in the sentences below should begin with capital letters? Why?

1. I visited houston in texas.
2. My aunt lives in chicago, illinois.
3. Is st. louis in missouri?
4. While you were in ohio, did you see cleveland?

For Practice

Written A. Write these words. Each names a city or a state. Use capital letters where they are needed.

1. danbury
2. troy
3. newark
4. chicago
5. modesto
6. connecticut
7. new york
8. new jersey
9. illinois
10. california

For More Practice
See Page 319

B. Write the sentences below. Use capital letters where they are needed. Use commas and periods, too.

1. He lives in milwaukee, wisconsin.
2. She flew to detroit, michigan.
3. When in iowa, visit des moines.
4. You may see us in st. paul, minnesota.

9. For Review

Read and discuss the questions below.

A. Which group of words below has three sounds spelled with three letters? Which has three sounds spelled with four letters? What words can you add to each group?

1	2
tap	maid
net	bear
bun	bell

B. Which sentence below is a statement? Which is a *yes/no* question? How did you decide?

1. The car is new.   **2.** Are you ready to go?

C. How would you change each sentence in group *1* below to a *yes/no* question? How would you change each *yes/no* question in group *2* to a statement?

1	2
The cookies are good.	Are the pears ripe?
The girls like the car.	Do the boys like apples?
The boys saw a giraffe.	Did the boys eat the pie?

D. What kind of letter is used to begin each name below? Why?

Streets	Schools	Cities	States
Elm Street	Emerson School	Dallas	Texas
Third Avenue	Garfield School	Trenton	New Jersey
Willow Road	Bailey School	Richmond	Virginia

Read the directions for each exercise below. Follow the directions, writing your answers on your own paper.

A. Change these statements to *yes/no* questions beginning with *is* or *are*.

1. The party is fun.
2. The fish are biting.
3. Breakfast is ready.
4. The kittens are hungry.

B. Change these statements to *yes/no* questions beginning with *do* or *did*.

5. The boys like movies.
6. The children played games.
7. The mothers made costumes.

C. Change the following *yes/no* questions to statements.

8. Is the house clean?
9. Do the leaves look brown?
10. Did the boys win prizes?

D. For each name below, write the letter or letters in it that you think should be a capital letter.

11. dempster street	14. tampa
12. batavia avenue	15. new york
13. adair school	16. linn road

11. Talking about Life at Home

Look at each picture. Then answer these questions.

- Where are these people?

- Which of the two persons in each picture would you rather be? Why?

Have you done something at home that made you feel a little foolish at the time? These questions may help you remember one of the things.

1. Have you ever eaten something that you thought was something else?
2. Have you played a trick that went wrong?
3. Have you worn someone else's clothes by mistake?
4. Have you wakened your family too early?

Activities

A. Think of something you did at home that made you feel foolish at the time. Choose something that seems funny now. Think of what you might say to tell someone about it.

B. Divide into groups of about four people in each group. Try these activities.

1. Sit together and take turns telling about things that happened to you at home. Tell about things that seem funny now. Be sure to tell how each thing happened. Tell what you did and what you said. Tell what the other family members did and said. Also tell how you felt about what happened.
2. The members of your group may pick two of the stories to tell to the class. Maybe your group will want to act out a story as it is being told.
3. Your class may want to choose two or three stories to tell the other classes. Perhaps you might invite the other classes to visit yours.

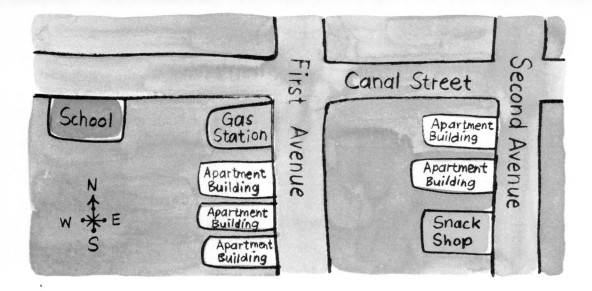

12. Giving Directions

Listen as your teacher reads the following directions. See if you can follow them on the map.

My home is in an apartment on First Avenue. To get there from school, go out the front door. Go east on Canal Street to the gas station at Canal and First. Turn south on First Avenue. Go past the first two apartment buildings. I live in the third one.

Go back and read the directions again. Think about the directions. As you do so, answer these questions.

- Which sentence names the street where the home is?

- Which sentence tells where the walk begins?

- Which sentence tells where the direction of the walk changes?

- Which sentence tells where to stop?

Suppose that you were going to tell a person how to reach the snack shop shown on the map. What does he need to know in order to find it?

A. Your class may find or make a map of the neighborhood near your school. Show the school. Also show some places to name when you give directions.

B. Decide if your home can be shown on the map. If so, give directions to your home. Try giving them to a person who does not know where your home is. He is to try to find it on the map. Be sure to answer these questions.

1. What is the address of your home?
2. What is the starting point for the person?
3. Which way will the person go when he starts out?
4. What turns will the person make?
5. How will he know when he is at each turn?
6. How will he know when he reaches your home?

C. If your home cannot be shown on the map, do this. Make a map that someone could use to find your home. Then choose someone who doesn't know where your home is. Give him directions to your home. Ask him to find your home on the map.

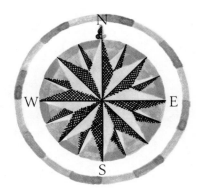

55

13. Writing Stories

The author of these stories made believe that he was a pet living with people in their home. Read these stories. What did the animal do in each story? Why did he do what he did?

My family likes to watch television as its favorite thing to do. Some programs have sirens that shriek. I whine and bark to make them turn the set off.

My family's house is quietest early in the morning. The tick-tick-tick of the clock and the drip-drip-drip of a leaky faucet break the stillness. Then I bark to get a pleasant sound in the house.

A. Does your family like to do one thing better than anything else? Does it have a favorite food? Is there something special about your home at different times of the day?

B. Pretend that an animal who lives in a home can tell about things as he sees them happen. Talk about what the animal might say.

Activities

A. Think of something that an animal might say about your family. Write a story about it. These sentences may give you ideas for the first sentence of your story. You may want to think of your own first sentence.

1. My family likes to travel better than anything else.
2. My family likes to eat apple pie better than anything else.
3. My home is quietest early in the morning.
4. My home is very noisy in the evening.

Your second sentence might tell what the animal saw or heard. Your last sentence might tell what the animal did.

B. Draw a picture for your story. Show the picture as you read your story for a friend or for the class.

C. Perhaps you can put your stories and pictures up in your room for others to look at. First copy each story over to make it look as nice as you can.

14. Making a Postcard

What kinds of things do you expect to see on Halloween? What kinds of things happen then?

Look at the postcard which a girl made for her mother after looking at Halloween pictures.

- ■ What was the girl's name?

- ■ What did she see in the Halloween pictures that gave her an idea for her picture? For her poem?

- ■ What did she say in the address? Where did she write it?

Dear Mother,

 I wrote this poem for you.

Halloween witches fly
  through the night,
With cats
And bats
And ghosts all white.

   Mary

Mrs. Wayne Tall
145 Arthur Street
Elmhurst, Ill. 60126

What are some things you might see on Halloween? What words could you use in telling where you saw them? What words might you use in telling what they did? What words might you use in telling how they looked?

Activities

A. Cut out a piece of thin cardboard you can use as a postcard. You may want to make a giant-sized card.

B. Make up a message for a friend. Part of the message should be a poem. These things may help you think of what to say in your poem.

1. Think of things you might see on Halloween.
2. Think of words that tell about the things.

C. Make a picture for your poem. Put it on the front of your postcard.

D. Address your card. Either mail it or take it home.

59

15. Listening to Poetry

Listen as your teacher reads the following poem to you.

GODFREY GORDON GUSTAVUS GORE

Godfrey Gordon Gustavus Gore—
No doubt you have heard the name before—
Was a boy who never would shut a door!

The wind might whistle, the wind might roar,
And teeth be aching and throats be sore,
But still he never would shut the door.

His father would beg, his mother implore,
"Godfrey Gordon Gustavus Gore,
We really *do* wish you would shut the door!"

Their hands they wrung, their hair they tore;
But Godfrey Gordon Gustavus Gore
Was deaf as the buoy out at the Nore.

When he walked forth the folks would roar,
"Godfrey Gordon Gustavus Gore,
Why don't you think to shut the door?"

They rigged out a Shutter with sail and oar,
And threatened to pack off Gustavus Gore
On a voyage of penance to Singapore.

But he begged for mercy, and said, "No more!
Pray do not send me to Singapore
On a Shutter, and then I will shut the door!"

"You will?" said his parents; "then keep on shore!
But mind you do! For the plague is sore
Of a fellow that never will shut the door,
Godfrey Gordon Gustavus Gore!"

—WILLIAM BRIGHTY RANDS

Listen as your teacher reads the poem again. Be ready to answer these questions.

- Do you think the poet wanted you to have fun with this poem? Why?
- What kind of boat would a shutter make?

For Discussion

Read aloud parts of the poem which help answer the following questions.

1. How do you know that his parents were upset with Godfrey? Read lines from the poem to prove your answer.

2. How do you know that the mother and father really intended to break Godfrey's bad habit? What lines from the poem tell you this?

3. Was the plan to break Godfrey's bad habit any good? What lines from the poem tell you this?

Activities

A. Draw a picture of the boat.

B. Find another poem that you think is funny. Give your poem to someone to read.

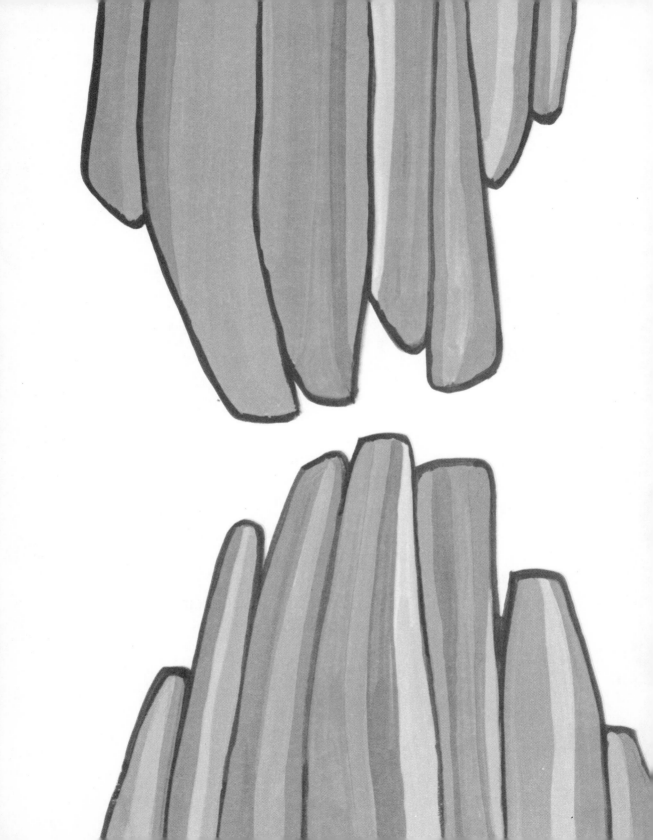

CHAPTER 3

1. Names of Days
2. Words That Sound Alike
3. Words That Look Alike
4. Two Kinds of Questions
5. Questions Beginning with *Who* or *How*
6. Writing the Names of Days and Months
7. Writing Names of Special Days
8. For Review
9. For Testing
10. Talking about School
11. Playing a Role
12. Writing a Cheer-up Letter
13. Writing a Letter to a Make-believe Friend
14. Listening to Poetry

1. Names of Days

The picture shows one of the gods some people believed in long ago. The god's name was Thor. He was the god of lightning and thunder.

"A god as strong as this ought to have a day of his own," some people said. So they named a day after him. They called it *Thor's day*. What is the name of that day now?

64

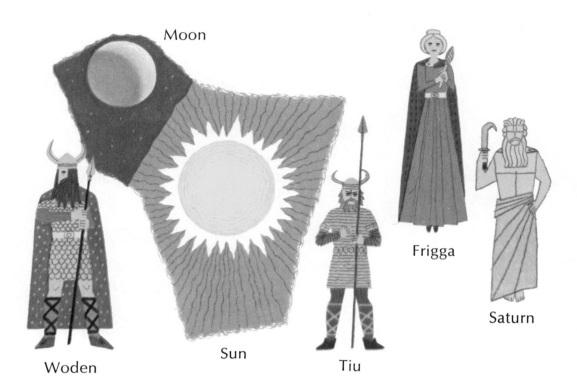

Moon

Woden

Sun

Tiu

Frigga

Saturn

Each person and thing shown above had a day named after it. Read the name below each picture. Use the word *day* with each name. Then answer these questions.

- What was each day called?
- What are our names for these days?

For Discussion

A. What day of the week is named for each person or thing below?

1. Tiu   3. Woden   5. Frigga   7. Thor
2. Moon   4. Sun   6. Saturn

B. What new names would you like to invent for the days of the week?

2. Words That Sound Alike

Listen as you read the sentence below softly to yourself. Do the words shown in color sound alike?

Neal won one prize.

Look again at the words in color above. Then answer these questions.

- What letters are used to spell each word?
- Do these two words have the same meaning?
  Or do the words have different meanings?

English has many other words like *won* and *one*. They sound alike, but they are not spelled alike. They have different meanings, too.

See if you can think of words like the ones that you have read about.

A. What word can you think of to name each picture below? How should each word be spelled? What sentence can you make using each word?

B. What other words can you think of that sound like the words you used to name the pictures? These words should be spelled differently. They should have different meanings. What sentences can you make using these words?

ON YOUR OWN

Make a collection of words that sound the same but have different spellings. Your class might like to have a contest to see who can make the longest list.

3. Words That Look Alike

Read the sentence in the box softly to yourself. Do the words shown in color sound alike?

> The wind can wind a flag around a flagpole.

Look again at the words shown in color in the sentence in the box. Say the words softly to yourself.

- Which word rhymes with *mind?*
- Which word rhymes with *pinned?*

Now study the two words shown in color in the sentence in the box.

- What letters are used to spell each word?
- Do the words have the same meaning? Or do they have different meanings?

English has a number of other words that are spelled the same. They do not sound alike when you use them in sentences. They do not have the same meaning, either.

See if you can think of any words like the ones that you have read about.

What sentences can you make up using each word below?

1. does (rhymes with *buzz*)

2. does (rhymes with *goes*)

3. lead (rhymes with *need*)

4. lead (rhymes with *bed*)

5. live (rhymes with *give*)

6. live (rhymes with *hive*)

7. tear (rhymes with *here*)

8. tear (rhymes with *hair*)

ON YOUR OWN

See if you can find out the meanings of two words that are spelled *b-a-s-s*. Draw a picture to show what each word means. Ask a friend to write a sentence for each picture. He must use the word *bass* in each sentence.

4. Two Kinds of Questions

Read the three sentences below. Are they statements or questions? How can you tell?

> Did Jane fix the chairs?
>
> When did Jane fix the chairs?
>
> Where did Jane fix the chairs?

Compare the three sentences above.

- Which words are the same?

- Which sentence is a *yes/no* question? How can you tell?

- What answer does the second sentence ask for?

- What answer does the third sentence ask for?

- What two letters begin the words *when* and *where?*

One kind of question is a *yes/no* question. The other kind is called a **wh-question**. Why do you think questions beginning with *when* or *where* are called *wh*-questions? How are *yes/no* and *wh*-questions different in the answers they ask for?

A. Which question below is a *yes/no* question? Which questions are *wh*-questions? How do you know?

1. Did you lose your dog?
2. Where did you lose your dog?
3. When did you lose your dog?

B. What *yes/no* questions and *wh*-questions might the boy shown below ask the man?

For Practice

For More Practice
See Page 320

Oral Turn each question below into two *wh*-questions. Have one of the sentences begin with *when*. Have the other begin with *where*.

1. Did you buy some gum?
2. Did you lose a pencil?
3. Did you find that book?
4. Is Mary Ann going?
5. Did you see the turtle?

Written Write two *wh*-questions for each *yes/no* question below. Begin the first question with *when*. Begin the second question with *where*.

1. Did you lose a button?
2. Did you find the quarter?
3. Did you buy pop?
4. Did you see a red truck?
5. Did you see a giraffe?

5. Questions Beginning with *Who* or *How*

Read the statement and the question below. Compare the two sentences.

> Jan bought peanut butter.
> Who bought peanut butter?

- Which words are the same?
- Which words are different?
- What is the answer to the question?
- What two letters begin the word *who*?

A question that begins with *who* is a *wh*-question. What other *wh*-question can you think of that begins with *who*? Now compare the two questions below.

> Did Howard fix the tire?
> How did Howard fix the tire?

- Which words in the questions are the same?
- Which sentence is a *yes/no* question?

The second question also is called a *wh*-question even though it begins with *how*. What other *wh*-questions can you think of that begin with *how*?

How are the sentences in each pair of sentences below alike? How are they different?

1. Doris caught an eel. Who caught an eel?

2. Did he fill the hole? How did he fill the hole?

For More Practice
See Page 320

Oral A. Change these statements into *wh*-questions that begin with *who*.

1. John brought sandwiches to the picnic.
2. Ann made some lemonade.
3. Julie put a box on the ground.
4. Mrs. Richards cut a watermelon.
5. Everyone ate the food.

B. Turn each question below into a *wh*-question beginning with *how*.

1. Did you light the fire?
2. Did Jane fix the lock?
3. Did Doris make the apron?
4. Do you make pancakes?
5. Do boys and girls climb trees?

ON YOUR OWN

Play an alphabet question-and-answer game about a make-believe picnic. The game goes like this.

1ST PLAYER: I brought **a**pples. Who brought **b**read?

2ND PLAYER: Ann brought **b**read. Who brought **c**heese?

The players are supposed to work their way through the alphabet. A player who cannot think of a question loses his turn.

Days of the Week	Months of the Year	
Sunday	January	July
Monday	February	August
Tuesday	March	September
Wednesday	April	October
Thursday	May	November
Friday	June	December
Saturday		

6. Writing the Names of Days and Months

Read the name of each day and of each month.

■ What kind of letter is used to begin the name of each day? Of each month?

For Discussion

Tell what changes you would make in each sentence below. Tell why you would make them.

1. People vote on the first tuesday in november.
2. We have gym on monday and friday.
3. School begins in september and ends in june.

For Practice

Written Write the answer to each question. Use capital letters where they are needed.

1. Which names of days have six letters?
2. Which names of days have eight letters?

For More Practice
See Page 321

3. Which names of months end with *ber?*

4. Which names of months end with *ary?*

5. Which names have fewer letters than *August?*

74

7. Writing Names of Special Days

Find the names of special days on the posters.

■ What kind of letter is used to begin each word in the name of a special day?

Explain how the following names should be written.
1. independence day   2. washington's birthday

For More Practice
See Page 321

Written Write the name of each special day. Use capital letters where they belong.

1. memorial day
2. halloween
3. united nations day
4. groundhog day
5. new year's day
6. good friday
7. columbus day
8. labor day
9. christmas day
10. yom kippur

75

8. For Review

Read and discuss the questions below.

A. Which words below sound alike but are spelled differently? Which words are spelled alike but do not sound alike? What pairs of such words can you add?

son   sun   bow   bow

B. Which question below is a *yes/no* question? Which is a *wh*-question? How did you decide?

1. Do you like pears?   **2.** Who likes pears?

C. What *wh*-questions can you make from these statements? Use *who* to begin your questions.

1. Manuel plays the piano.   **2.** They played games.

D. What *wh*-questions can you make from these *yes/no* questions? Use *when* or *where* to begin your questions.

1. Did Ann go to Arizona?   **2.** Did Ann go last week?

E. Why are capital letters used to begin these words?

1. Sunday   **2.** December   **3.** Labor Day
     Monday   June   Columbus Day

76

Read the directions for each exercise below. Follow the directions, writing your answers on your own paper.

A. Change each *wh*-question below to a *yes/no* question.

1. When did Sue do her homework?
2. Where did Julie find her kitten?
3. When did Glenn tear his jacket?

B. Change each statement below to a *wh*-question. Begin each *wh*-question with *who*.

4. Martha made some cookies.
5. The children went to the zoo.
6. Tina likes to play checkers.

C. Change each *yes/no* question below to a *wh*-question. Begin the *wh*-questions with the words in ( ).

7. Did Sandra write a letter yesterday? (when)
8. Did Charles go home? (where)

D. Write the names of the special days below. Use capital letters where you need them.

9. independence day
10. halloween

Dwight Ellefsen

Rohn Engh

10. Talking about School

The girls and boys are at school. What kinds of things are they doing? Which of the things have you done in your school? What other things do you do at school?

Make plans to invite your mothers to your room. These questions may help you plan.

1. What can you show your mothers? What can you say to them?

2. What can you do to invite your mothers?

Activities

A. On your own make something to show to your guests. Think of things to say about it.

B. Divide into groups of four or five pupils. Taking turns, tell what you would say to your mothers.

C. Write an invitation to give to your mother. The one below shows one way to do it.

Dear Mother,

    Please come to our classroom on Friday, October 25, from 2:00 p. m. to 3:30 p. m. We want to tell you about our school.

               Love,
               Marcia

11. Playing a Role

Read the poem and look at the picture beside it. Who was the teacher?

Who were the pupils?

TWENTY FROGGIES

Twenty froggies went to school
Down beside a rushy pool.
Twenty little coats of green,
Twenty vests all white and clean.

"We must be in time," said they,
"First we study, then we play;
That is how we keep the rule,
When we froggies go to school."

Master Bullfrog, brave and stern,
Called his classes in their turn,
Taught them how to nobly strive,
Also how to leap and dive;

Taught them how to dodge a blow,
From the sticks that bad boys throw.
Twenty froggies grew up fast,
Bullfrogs they became at last;

Polished in a high degree,
As each froggie ought to be,
Now they sit on other logs,
Teaching other little frogs.

—GEORGE COOPER

Read the poem again. Where did the frogs go to school? What did they learn at their school? What did they do with what they learned?

For Discussion

Talk about how you could act out a school planned for elephants or some other animals.

Activities

A. Form groups of five or six girls and boys in each group. Then try these activities.

1. Think of the kind of animal school your group would like to act out. Be sure to choose animals you know about.

2. Choose parts for each person to act out.

3. Talk about what each animal might do and what he might say. Also talk about what props your group needs.

4. Act out your roles more than once. Try to make your acting better each time.

B. Each group may put on its act for the rest of the class. Talk about how each act could be made better.

12. Writing a Cheer-up Letter

Dear Barbara,

How do you like our giraffe? His throat is sore just like yours. The cloth makes him feel better. Do you think a cloth would help you?

Yesterday your group had its school for giraffes. Every giraffe did neck-stretching exercises. Could you have done that?

Get well soon. Your group needs all of its giraffes. We need you, too.

Your Friends

Read the letter and answer these questions.

- Why did Barbara's friends write to her?

- What did they say to make Barbara feel that the letter was really for her?

- What did the letter say about school?

For Discussion

Suppose that you wanted to write a letter to a school friend who was too ill to talk to you.

1. What could you say to make your friend feel that the letter was just for him or her?

2. What could you say to help your friend keep up-to-date about school?

3. What could you say to cheer up your friend?

Activities

A. Form groups of two members each.

1. Each partner is to make believe that the other one is ill at home. The partners may write letters to each other.

2. The partners may exchange letters and read them just for fun. Then they might check the letters for spelling, capital letters, and periods.

B. Have fun reading some of the letters in class. The class may choose some letters to put on a bulletin board.

13. Writing a Letter to a Make-believe Friend

The writer of this letter made believe that she had an ant as her friend.

Read the letter to yourself. Find out what the writer knew about her friend.

Dear Friendly Ant,

We had a party at school. I was looking for you. I know how parties please you.

You would have liked the end of the party best. That's when we ate. I dropped some crumbs of cake for you.

I'll let you know when our next party comes. Don't miss it.

Love,
Sandy

Sandy let her friend know that she knew what her friend liked. What did Sandy say in order to do this?

Talk about things you might say in a letter to each of these animal friends that missed a school party.

1. A spider that liked to eat flies
2. A white mouse that liked people's pockets
3. A bee that liked sweet things
4. A crow that liked shiny things

A. By yourself you might enjoy this.

1. Think of an animal friend who might like to get a letter from you.
2. Write the friend a letter. Say something that makes him feel that you know something he likes.

B. Choose a partner and exchange letters with him. Both of you may check the letters for spelling, capital letters, and periods. Write your letter again to make it look better.

C. Make a picture of the animal friend you chose. Put your picture and your letter on the bulletin board.

85

14. Listening to Poetry

Listen as your teacher reads this poem to you.

THIS MAN CAME FROM NOWHERE

I took a lump of clay in my hand
And patted and pricked it and pulled it AND
There was a man!—with a bump of a head
And two long legs! He winked and said:
"You forgot my ears. You forgot my nose.
You forgot my hands. And, I suppose,
I could think of other things you forgot,
But I don't mind, for I like you a lot,
And I'm glad as can be that you made me this
    way
Out of nothing at all but a lump of clay.
Now try another, and see if you can
Make not just *some*, but *all* of a man."

—JOHN CIARDI

Listen as your teacher reads the poem again. Be ready to answer these questions.

- Is the poet telling about a real man or a make-believe man?

- Does the poet make you like the man? Or does he make you dislike him?

For Discussion

Read aloud the parts of the poem which help you answer the following questions.

1. What did the poet do to make the man?

2. How did the man look? What lines tell you?

3. How do you know that the man liked the poet? What word in the poem is your first clue? What lines tell you that the man liked the poet?

Activities

A. Form groups of two. One person may take the part of the poet who wrote the poem. The other may take the part of the man. Act out the poem for the class.

B. Make a man out of clay. Write a sentence telling what your clay man might like to say to you.

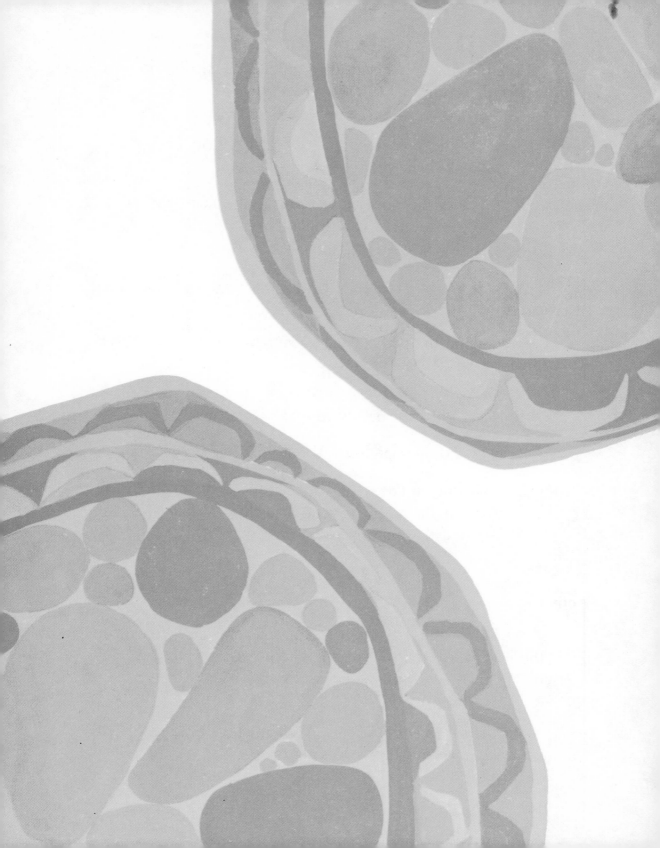

CHAPTER 4

1. Names of Months

The names for the months are very old. Some of the months were named after Roman gods and goddesses. To find out who they were, read the names in each group below.

- Who were January and March named after?
- Who was May named after?

Some months were named after people. Find out who they were by reading these names.

- Who were June and July named after?
- Who was August named after?

Count the dots in each box below and read the words below the dots. These words are names that the Romans used for numbers.

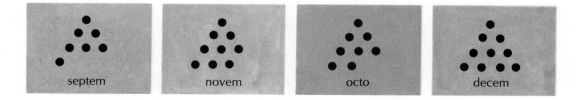

septem   novem   octo   decem

■ What number does each word name?

■ Which four months were named after numbers?

Read the names in the two groups below.

FEBRUA (A holiday)

February

APRILIS (A word meaning "to open")

April

■ What was February named after?

■ What was April named after?

For Discussion

What new names would you like to invent for months? What plan might you use if you named them after numbers?

2. Syllables

Listen as you say the first word in the box below. It has one group of speech sounds.

Listen as you say the second word in the box. It has two groups of speech sounds.

pop	popcorn	can	candy	ten	tender

Each separate group of sounds in a word is called a **syllable.** Some words have one syllable. Some words have two or more syllables.

Look at the words in the box again.

- How many syllables does *can* have?

- How many syllables does *candy* have?

- Which three words have one syllable?

- Which three words have two syllables?

Think about what you have learned. How can you tell if a word has more than one syllable?

For Discussion

A. Which words below have one syllable? How can you tell?

1. up	**3.** garden	**5.** butter
2. upset	**4.** car	**6.** house

B. Which words below have more than one syllable? How can you tell?

1. birthday	**3.** change	**5.** would
2. morning	**4.** mother	**6.** father

92

Oral Think of a name to go with each picture below. Say each of the names. Tell whether each name has one syllable or two.

1.

2.

3.

4.

5.

6.

7.

8.

9.

ON YOUR OWN

Write the first names of five people. Choose names that have only one syllable. Give your list to a partner. See if your partner thinks that each name has only one syllable.

3. Stress

Each word below has two syllables. Listen as you say each word softly to yourself.

bal loon

bas ket

- Do you give the same amount of force to each syllable? Or do you say one syllable more loudly than the other? If so, which one?

The amount of force or loudness that you give to a syllable when you say it has a name. This name is **stress.** Which syllable in *basket* receives the greater stress?

For Discussion

A. How would you explain what stress is?

B. Which syllable receives the greater stress in each of the following words?

1. rab bit   3. al so   5. frost ing

2. les son   4. pan cake   6. drag on

Oral Think of a syllable to go with each syllable below. The word you make should go with the picture.

Say each word you make. Tell which syllable in your word receives the greater stress.

1. ba–

2. ca–

3. mon–

5. ap–

6. ham–

4. blan–

7. a–

8. gi–

9. ga–

10. cam–

95

4. The Two Parts of a Sentence

Read each of the sentences below in two parts. Do this by stopping after reading the part in color. Then read the other part.

The chain broke.

A man fixed the chain.

The chain was like new again.

You can divide all English sentences like those above into two parts. One part names *who* or *what* the sentence is about. This part is the **subject.** The other part tells what this person or thing *does*, or *did*, or *is*, or *was*. This part is the **predicate**.

Read the example sentences again.

- What is the subject in each sentence?
- What is the predicate in each sentence?
- Which part comes first, the subject or the predicate?
- Which part comes second, the subject or the predicate?

Think about what you have learned. What two parts do sentences like those about the chain have? Which part comes first? What does each part tell?

Which sentence below the pictures has been divided correctly into subject and predicate? Which has not? How can you tell?

The | girl is late.

The man | was too hot.

For More Practice
See Page 321

**For
Practice**

Oral A. Add a subject to each predicate below to make a sentence.

1. — flew away.
2. — ate a pear.
3. — hid in a tree.
4. — was in his pocket.
5. — sat on a rock.

B. Add a predicate to each subject below to make a sentence.

1. The tired boy —.
2. Some water —.

3. Monkeys —.
4. A hungry lion —.
5. Ice-cream cones —.

Written Make some meaningful sentences by matching each subject with one of the predicates. Write the sentences.

1. The robin   swam away.
2. Two fish   barked.
3. My friend   is about trucks.
4. The dog   ate a worm.
5. The book   talked to me.

97

5. Adding Predicates

Read these sentences about the wind. First read the subject part and then read the predicate part of each sentence.

Subjects	Predicates
The wind	rumbles like an ocean.
The wind	whispers in the windows.
The wind	howls through the trees.

- What is the subject of each sentence?

- Are the subjects the same or are they different?

- What is the predicate of each sentence?

- Are the predicates the same or are they different?

Read the sentences in the box again. Can the same subject be used with only one predicate? Or can the same subject be used with many different predicates?

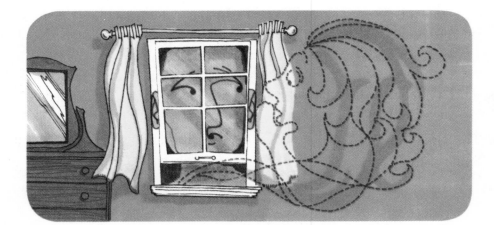

What sentences can you think of that begin with the subject below each picture?

The little kangaroo—.

The salted peanuts—.

The noisy truck—.

For More Practice
See Page 322

**For
Practice**

Oral Make sentences by thinking of two or more predicates for each subject below. Say your sentences aloud.

1. The hungry kitten —.
2. The ragged boy —.
3. Two little frogs —.
4. Our friends —.
5. My yellow pencil —.
6. The old umbrella —.
7. The truck driver —.
8. A baby rabbit —.
9. My new pair of shoes —.
10. The big black clouds —.

Written Make up sentences by adding two different predicates to each subject below. Write your sentences.

1. My bicycle —.
2. The builder —.
3. A young painter —.
4. A snapping turtle —.
5. The bright sun —.

99

6. Adding Subjects

Subjects	Predicates
The white snow	blew away.
My new kite	blew away.
The maple leaves	blew away.

Read the sentences in the box above.

- What is the subject of each sentence?
- Are the subjects the same or different?
- What is the predicate of each sentence?
- Are the predicates the same or different?

Read the sentences in the box again. Can the same predicate be used with only one subject? Or can the same predicate be used with many different subjects?

For Discussion

What subjects can you add to each predicate below?

1. — walked in space.
2. — jumped the fence easily.
3. — helped the child across the street.
4. — barked all day.
5. — lay on the ground.

For More Practice
See Page 322

Oral Make sentences by thinking of two different subjects for each predicate below. Say your sentences aloud.

1. — hangs on a hook.

2. — painted a door.

3. — worked in a mine.

4. — rolled over and over.

5. — sold us a car.

6. — floated away.

7. — eats too much candy.

8. — smiles at her friends.

9. — hops up and down.

10. — is thinking of something.

Written Add a different subject to each predicate below. Each subject must have two or more words. Write your sentences.

1. — saw the shining moon.

2. — saw the shining moon.

3. — saw the shining moon.

4. — ran across the street.

5. — ran across the street.

6. — ran across the street.

7. — sailed over the fence.

8. — sailed over the fence.

9. — rolled into a corner.

10. — rolled into a corner.

ON YOUR OWN

Make four sentences by adding two different subjects to each predicate below the colors.

— is green.   — are red.

7. Writing Dates

Look at the date on each of the clippings. Then answer these questions.

- What is the month and day?

- What kind of letter begins the name of the month?

- What is the year?

Find the punctuation mark in the date April 15, 1900. It is called a **comma.** Where is a comma used in a date?

For Discussion

Where would you use a comma in these dates?

1. October 12 1492

2. July 4 1776

3. January 1 1990

4. February 12 1809

For Practice

Written Write these sentences. Replace each of the blanks with a date. Give the month, day, and year. Use a calendar if you need to.

1. Today is —.

2. The date of my birthday is —.

3. School began on —.

4. Last Monday, the date was —.

5. Our next holiday comes on —.

102

8. Capital Letters in Story Titles

How does each word in these story titles begin?

Playful Yellow Kitten

Mystery in the Night

Read the two story titles again. Answer these questions.

- Which words in each title are the most important?
- What kind of letter begins each important word?

Think about writing story titles. What would you do to show which words are the most important?

For Discussion

Which words in each story title below would you begin with a capital letter? Why?

1. cricket in the clock
2. riding on a camel
3. treasure by a railroad

For Practice

For More Practice
See Page 322

Written Write each story title below. Use capital letters where they are needed.

1. two lost pennies
2. letter for susan

3. new pair of shoes

4. key to a mystery

5. bad day for geese

6. house on the tracks

9. For Review

Read and discuss the questions below.

A. Which words below have only one syllable? Which words have more than one syllable? How can you tell?

puppet

horse

lion

man

B. Say the words below. Which syllable in each word receives the greater stress? How do you know?

    1. football   **2.** garage   **3.** peanut

C. Which group below, *1* or *2*, can you use as subjects? As predicates? How can you make the words in each group into sentences?

    1. the boys   **2.** rode on a camel

         Alan and Joe   went to the zoo

         a hungry kitten   liked his supper

D. Which words below would you begin with capital letters? Why? Where would you put a comma in the date?

peter towers   november 5   197—

             make way for stevie

stevie was the youngest of the boys in the family.

Read the directions for each exercise below. Follow the directions, writing your answers on your own paper.

A. Write **1** or **2** for each name below to show the number of syllables in that name.

1. Mike   **2.** Stanley   **3.** Marie

B. Write **first** or **second** for each word below to show which syllable receives the greater stress.

4. noisy   **5.** below   **6.** puzzle

C. For each word group below, write **S** or **P**. Write **S** if the word group can be used as the subject of a sentence. Write **P** if it can be used as the predicate.

7. won a prize

8. the goldfish

9. woke up the whole family

10. the youngest kitten

11. all the pets

D. Write these dates. Put commas where they are needed.

12. July 4 1776   **13.** October 12 1492

E. Write these story titles. Use capital letters where they are needed.

14. angela wins again   **15.** secrets of the wizard

11. Talking about Indoor Games

CHECKERS

BLIND MAN'S BUFF

SPEAR THE RING

Look at the games shown in the pictures. Then answer these questions.

- What is the name of each game?
- Which game could you play alone?
- Which game could you play with one person?
- Which game is played by a group of persons?
- Would you like some other game better than any of the games shown in the pictures? If so, why?

For Discussion

A. Make believe that you can play one of the three games. Then answer these questions.

1. Which game would you choose? Why?
2. What kinds of things do you need to play the game? Where could you get these things?

B. What rules must you know in order to play Checkers?

C. In what places could you play Blind Man's Buff? What rules would be the same in each place? What rules might be different?

D. What rules would be good rules for playing Spear the Ring?

E. What is another good game to play indoors? What do you like about the game?

12. Explaining a Group Game

Have you ever played the game explained below? If so, did you play it in the same way? Read the explanation to find out.

MUSICAL CHAIRS

This game needs a piano or a record player. It also needs one less chair than there are players. The chairs are placed as shown in the picture.

The players join hands to make a chain around the chairs. When the music begins, the players drop hands and march around the chairs. Then the music stops. Everyone tries to sit on a chair. The player who does not get a chair must leave the game.

Then one of the chairs is taken away and the game begins again. The game continues until there is only one chair left. The person who gets to sit in this chair wins the game.

Read the explanation again. Does it leave out anything that a player needs to know?

For Discussion

A. Why must all of these things be in any explanation of a game?

1. The things to use
2. How the game begins
3. What the leader does
4. What the players do
5. How the game ends

B. How would you explain each of these games?

1. Button, Button
2. Pin the Tail on the Donkey

Activities

Divide into groups of four or five people.

1. Think of an indoor game the others do not know.
2. Explain the game to members of your group.
3. The group might want to play the game you explain.

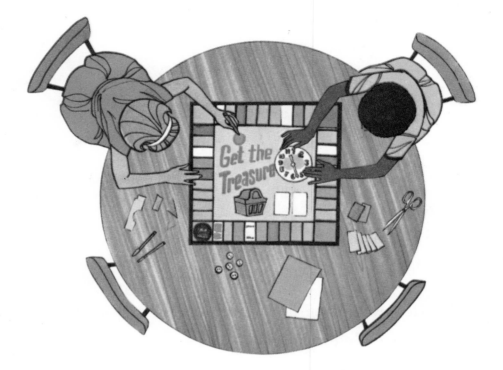

13. Writing Rules for a Game

These two girls have made up a game of their own.

- What did they name the game?
- What will they do with the spinner?
- How will they use the buttons?

The girls made up rules for their game. Here are two of the rules. What other rules might they need?

1. Each player may spin the spinner. The first player to get a *1* begins the game.

2. Only one button can be on a space at one time.

Make up more rules for the game the girls made up. These questions may help you think of rules.

1. How many players can the game have?

2. Who can be the second player?

3. How can a player tell how far to move his marker on each turn?

4. How can players keep from having two markers on one space?

5. How is a winner chosen?

Activities

A. Work with three or four partners.

1. Make up a game in which a game board is used. Make up a name for your game. Make the game board, too.

2. Write the rules you think you will need for your game.

3. Try to play the game you made up. Change any rules that are poor rules. Make up more rules if you need to.

B. Change games with another group of pupils. Each group might try to play the game it gets. Change any of the rules if you need to.

C. The class may vote to decide which games they like best.

D. Some of you might want to put the games in the game corner of your room.

14. Telling about a Homemade Game

The boy has made up a game that he calls Tip the Bottle. Why is that a good name?

Now read the story about the game. Who is doing the talking?

Tip the Bottle

I was the only bottle in a box. A boy came and got me. He set me on the kitchen floor. Then he took a three-foot string with a ring tied to it. He tied this string to a stick. The boy stood about five feet from me and tried to hook the ring on my neck. When he did this, he tipped me over. Then he called his brother. They took turns trying to tip me over. The boy who tipped me over first shouted, "I won! I won!"

Go back and read about the game again. What would you have to do to get ready to play Tip the Bottle? How would you play the game?

Hole in One

How many times in a row
can you catch the ball?

Suppose that you were the tin can at the end of the stick. What could you say to help someone learn about Hole in One?

A. Make a game to put in a game corner in your room. Your game might be something like Tip the Bottle or Hole in One. It might be a game played with jar rings and a board like this. Write a name for your game.

B. Write a story to put with your game. Tell the story as something in the game might tell it.

C. Show your game and your story to some friends. Try playing your game with them.

114

15. Listening to Poetry

Listen as your teacher reads the following poem to you.

"ONE, TWO, THREE!"

It was an old, old, old, old lady,
    And a boy that was half-past three;
And the way that they played together
    Was beautiful to see.

She couldn't go romping and jumping,
    And the boy no more could he;
For he was a thin little fellow,
    With a thin little twisted knee.

They sat in the yellow sunlight,
    Out under the maple tree;
And the game they played I'll tell you,
    Just as it was told to me.

It was hide-and-go-seek they were playing,
    Though you'd never have known it to be—
With an old, old, old, old lady,
    And a boy with a twisted knee.

The boy would bend his face down
    On his little sound right knee,
And he guessed where she was hiding
    In guesses One, Two, Three.

"You are in the china closet!"
    He would laugh and cry with glee—
It wasn't the china closet,
    But he still had Two and Three.

"You are up in Papa's big bedroom,
    In the chest with the queer old key!"
And she said: "You are *warm* and *warmer*;
    But you're not quite right," said she.

"It can't be the little cupboard
    Where Mamma's things used to be—
So it must be in the clothes press, Gran'ma!"
    And he found her with his Three.

Then she covered her face with her fingers,
    That were wrinkled and white and wee,
And she guessed where the boy was hiding,
    With a One and a Two and a Three.

And they never had stirred from their places
    Right under the maple tree—
This old, old, old, old lady,
    And the boy with the lame little knee—
This dear, dear, dear old lady,
    And the boy who was half-past three.

—HENRY CUYLER BUNNER

Listen as your teacher reads the poem again. As you listen, think about the answers to these questions.

- Who are the two people named in the poem?

- Why did they invent a game?

- Why was the game such a good game for the two people?

For Discussion

Read aloud the parts of the poem which help answer the following questions.

1. Who are the people who made up the game?
2. Where did the people play their game?
3. How did the boy use each of his guesses?
4. What did the old lady do after the boy guessed her hiding place?

Activities

A. Try playing the game told about in the poem.

B. See if you can make up another game that the two people in the poem might have played. Choose a partner and try playing the game you made up.

C. Draw a picture to go with the game you made up.

117

CHAPTER 5

1. Names of Towns and Cities

Read the names on the camper. They tell places that the family visited.

- ■ Which name makes you think of an animal?

- ■ Which name makes you think of water?

- ■ Which name makes you think of mines?

- ■ Which name tells something about the land?

Have you been to towns or cities that have interesting names? Which of the names tell something about the place where the town or city is?

120

A. What reason might people have had for choosing the name of each town or city below?

1. Edgewood, Indiana
2. Springfield, Illinois
3. Foxhome, Minnesota
4. Goodview, Minnesota
5. Lakeside, Ohio
6. Alligator, Mississippi
7. Greentree, Pennsylvania
8. Highbank, Texas
9. Richland, Kansas
10. Copper Harbor, Michigan

B. What name might you give to a town or city at each place described below?

1. A place where broken arrows were found
2. A place where broken bows were found
3. A valley where buffalo live
4. A place on a bend in a river
5. A place on the side of a hill
6. A place that has coal
7. A place near a lake
8. A place near a field

ON YOUR OWN

A *ford* is a place where a river, stream, or other body of water is not too deep to cross by walking through the water. Use a map to find the names of five cities whose names end with *ford*. Decide which of those cities may once have had a ford. Write the names of those cities. Your class may wish to make a class list of all of the cities whose names end with *ford*.

2. Words with Similar Meanings

Read the sentences in each group below the picture.
Think about the meaning of each sentence.

1	2
The tiger is skinny.	The tiger will jump.
The tiger is scrawny.	The tiger will leap.
The tiger is lean.	The tiger will spring.

Read the sentences in group *1* again.

- Which words are the same?

- Which words are not the same?

- Are the sentences similar or different in meaning?

Now read the sentences in group *2*.

- Which words are the same?

- Which words are not the same?

- Are the sentences similar or different in meaning?

Words that have almost the same meaning are called **synonyms.** *Scrawny* is a synonym of *skinny*. *Leap* is a synonym of *jump*.

- What is another synonym of *skinny?*
- What is another synonym of *jump?*

Think about synonyms again. What sentence can you make that tells what synonyms are?

For Discussion

What synonyms could you use for the word in italics in each sentence below?

1. The boy *talked* to his sister.
2. The *big* bubble broke.
3. Geraldine's shoes were *soaked*.

For Practice

Oral Read each sentence below. Use a synonym in place of each word in italics.

1. Five *big* boys played Follow the Leader.
2. They *chose* John as the leader.
3. John *raced* to a fence.
4. He *squeezed* through a hole.
5. Then he leaped over a *small* wading pool.
6. A man *shouted* at John.
7. John stopped *quickly*.
8. He was *struck* by the boy behind him.
9. John *landed* in the water.
10. That *ended* the game.

Written Write each sentence below. Use a synonym in place of each word in italics.

1. Howard is a *big* boy.
2. Mary was *glad* to see her mother.
3. The bus moved *rapidly*.
4. The rose had *blooms* on it.
5. Alice will *toss* the ball to me.
6. Will you *speak* more softly?
7. Please *hop* over the fence.
8. Our house is *small*.

123

3. Words with Opposite Meanings

Read the poem. Then answer the questions below it.

I WANT TO GO TRAVELING

I want to go UP;
I want to go DOWN;
I want to go traveling
All around the town.

I want to go HERE;
I want to go THERE;
I want to see the Circus;
I want to see the Fair.

I want to go LEFT;
I want to go RIGHT;
I want to find acorns;
I want to fly a kite.

I want to go EAST;
I want to go WEST;
I want to lie down
For a good long rest.

—ILO ORLEANS

- What pairs of words are in capital letters?

- Are the words the same or are the words opposite in meaning?

124

Words that are opposite in meaning are called **antonyms.**
Down is an antonym of *up. There* is an antonym of *here.*
What are some other pairs of antonyms?

For Discussion

Which pairs of words below are antonyms? How can you tell?

1. happy—sad
2. hard—soft
3. large—small
4. high—tall

For Practice

Oral Read each question below. Then answer it with a statement beginning with *No.* Use an antonym in place of the word in italics.

1. Is the box *heavy?*
2. Are the clowns *foolish?*
3. Were the birds *wild?*
4. Was the boy *young?*
5. Is the knife *dull?*
6. Was the car *quiet?*
7. Is the dog *fat?*
8. Was the street *wet?*
9. Was the music *loud?*

ON YOUR OWN

Make up five statements and questions that have opposite meanings. Here is an example: *Ice is cold. What is hot?* Then play a game with them. The first player reads a statement and question. The player who answers first gets a turn to read a statement and question.

4. Nouns

girl   mouse   ship   house

Read the sentence below. Then answer the questions about it.

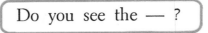

Do you see the — ?

■ Could you use each word below the pictures to complete the sentence?

■ What are some other words you could use to complete it?

The sentence *Do you see the — ?* is a test sentence. All of the words that fit the sentence are called **nouns.** Do you think that English has a great many or only a few nouns?

Which of the following words do you think are nouns? Use the test sentence to check your answer.

1. desk
2. pan
3. little

4. boy
5. many
6. flower

7. church
8. broke
9. sign

For Practice

For More Practice
See Page 323

Oral **A.** Say each sentence. Use a noun in place of each blank.

1. The little — barked.
2. That — is too sour.
3. My — was lost.
4. The — is cracked.

B. Say each sentence. Use a noun in place of each blank.

1. The — crawled on the —.
2. That — has one —.
3. The — fixed the —.
4. My — has a big —.

Written Write each sentence. Use a noun in place of each blank.

1. Our — is very old.
2. The big — ran.
3. His — is red.
4. The — is broken.
5. My — is loose.
6. Put the — in the house.
7. See the — in the tree.
8. My — has two pockets.
9. Our room has many —.
10. The door has one —.

127

5. Some Forms of Nouns

Read the words in the pictures above. Also read the test sentences. Then answer the questions below them.

Test Sentence 1

Do you see one —?

Test Sentence 2

Do you see two —?

- Could you use each word below the pictures to complete test sentence *1*?

- How would you have to change each word before you could use it to complete test sentence *2*?

Words that fit either test sentence are nouns. The words *boy* and *boys* are two forms of the same noun. What are two forms of *dog*? What are two forms of *box*?

The form of a noun that names one object or person is called the **singular form.** The form that names more than one object or person is called the **plural form.**

Now think about what you have discovered about the forms of nouns. What can you add to a noun to make it mean more than one object or person?

Which words below are singular nouns? Which are plural nouns? How can you tell?

1. erasers   3. fork   5. bees
2. trees   4. books   6. balloon

For More Practice
See Page 323

Oral A. Change each sentence below by putting *Two* in place of *The*. Check to make sure that each of the nouns becomes plural.

1. The bird sang in the morning.
2. The log drifted downstream.
3. The lake dried up.
4. The turtle swam away.
5. The plumber worked hard.

B. Change each sentence below by putting *One* in place of *The*. Check to make sure that each of the nouns becomes singular.

1. The bricklayers came.
2. The trucks had red wheels.
3. The bolts rusted.
4. The lions roared loudly.
5. The cars skidded.

Written A. Write each sentence below. Use the plural form of the noun in ( ).

1. These — were loaded with gravel. (truck)
2. The — were heavy. (box)
3. Two — went flat. (tire)
4. The — on the truck failed. (brake)
5. The boy saw two —. (circus)

B. Write each sentence below. Use the singular form of the noun in ( ).

1. The — had some candy. (girls)
2. The — was grounded. (jets)
3. The — grew fast. (trees)
4. The — was rusty. (nails)
5. His — had a dime. (brothers)

129

6. More Forms of Nouns

woman   child   man

Read the words in the picture above. Also read the test sentences. Then answer the questions below.

> **Test Sentences**
>
> **1.** Do you see one —?
> **2.** Do you see two —?

- Could you use each word to complete test sentence *1*? Try it.

- How would you have to change each word before you could use it to complete test sentence 2?

Now think of what you have discovered about the two forms of nouns. Do all plural nouns end in *s* or *es*?

For
Discussion

Read the words in each example below. Which words are singular? Which words are plural? How can you tell?

1. goose	geese	**6.** louse	lice
2. foot	feet	**7.** deer	deer
3. tooth	teeth	**8.** sheep	sheep
4. ox	oxen	**9.** man	men
5. mouse	mice	**10.** woman	women

For
Practice

For More Practice
See Page 323

Written Write each sentence. Use the plural form of the noun in ( ).

1. Those — are good workers. (man)
2. Two — are in the car. (woman)
3. My — are growing fast. (foot)
4. The — went home. (child)
5. His — are white. (tooth)
6. Five — flew by. (goose)
7. Two — pulled the wagon. (ox)
8. He caught three —. (mouse)
9. Two of the — are tiny. (deer)
10. The three — ran away. (sheep) 131

7. For Review

Read and discuss the questions below.

A. Which pairs of words below are synonyms? Which pairs are antonyms? How can you tell? What other synonyms and antonyms do you know?

1	2
speak—talk	happy—sad
large—big	young—old
glad—happy	big—little

B. Which of the words below are nouns? How can you use the test sentence in the box to help you decide?

> Do you see the —?

1. chair	**3.** found	**5.** violin
2. jacket	**4.** coat	**6.** listen

C. Which nouns below are singular? Which are plural? How can you tell?

1. spoons	**3.** crayon	**5.** foxes
2. bushes	**4.** flower	**6.** circuses

D. Do all plural nouns end in *s* or *es*? Use the noun forms below to help explain your answer. What nouns can you add to each list?

List 1		List 2	
Singular	**Plural**	**Singular**	**Plural**
boy	boys	woman	women
box	boxes	tooth	teeth

Read the directions for each exercise below. Follow the directions, writing your answers on your own paper.

A. For each pair of words below, write **synonyms** or **antonyms** to show what the words of that pair are.

1. tall—high   **3.** thick—thin

2. dry—wet   **4.** cry—weep

B. Decide which of the words in each pair below can be used as a noun. Use the test sentence below to help you decide. Then write the nouns.

5. liked, twins

6. package, happy

7. clouds, wet

8. tame, deer

> **Test Sentence**
>
> Do you see the —?

C. For each word below, write **singular** or **plural** to show what form of the noun each word is.

9. boat   **11.** geese

10. boxes   **12.** oxen

D. Write each sentence below. Use the plural form of the noun in ( ).

13. Sandra lost two (ticket).

14. The (child) helped find the turtle.

15. Did Stanley lose his (crayon)?

16. The (mouse) were out of their cages.

9. Talking about Outdoor Games

Children of all countries play games. One of the games played by the children of the Tuba Kasai tribe in the Congo is called Mubwabwa. A mubwabwa is a small antelope. Read the explanation of the game. See if you think you could play it.

MUBWABWA

This game is played on a field about the size of a tennis court. At least ten players are needed.

Someone is chosen to be *it*. He is the *mubwabwa*. He tries to catch the others. From time to time, he must shout "mubwabwa." The first player who is caught also shouts "mubwabwa." He helps the original mubwabwa. As other players are caught, they help the original mubwabwa, too. The last player to be caught wins the game.

Players cannot step out of the playing field.
Anyone who does is counted as being caught.

Read the explanation again. Then answer these questions about the game.

- How did the game get its name?
- What size should the playing field be?
- How many players are needed?
- How does the game begin?
- What are some rules of the game?

For Discussion

A. What are some other games that are running games and chasing games?

B. Which of your own running and chasing games are something like Mubwabwa? How are the games alike?

C. What is the first game or sport you think of when you hear each word below?

1. jumping
2. throwing
3. catching
4. kicking
5. sliding
6. skating

D. What kinds of things must you know about a new game before you can play it?

10. Writing a Story an Animal Might Tell

Read the following story. Who is doing the talking in it? What problems did he and his friends have in playing baseball?

A Strange Game

We porpoises had nothing to do one afternoon. "Let's play baseball," I said. Everyone agreed.

We found a rubber ball for our game. Then we laid out a diamond in the water, using leaves for bases. I was the pitcher. I tossed a ball to the first batter. He hit the ball with his head. The ball landed on second base and carried it away. The batter raced for first with his mouth open. As he hit the leaf, he snapped his jaws shut. That was the end of the base and of the game.

Read the story again. Then answer these questions about it.

- Who is doing the talking?
- What did the porpoises know about the game of baseball?
- What problems did the porpoises have with the bases?

Can you think of some other problems porpoises might have in the game of baseball? What might the problems be?

For Discussion

A. Talk about problems other animals might have if they could play games that people play. What problems might these animals have?

1. Deer that tried to ski
2. Kangaroos that tried to play football
3. Giraffes that tried to play basketball
4. Turtles that tried to water-ski

137

B. What sentences would you like to add to the story beginning below?

> We deer watched people flying down hills on flat boards. I heard a man say he was skiing. One day I found one of those boards. That night I went to the top of the hill. I put one foot on the board. Then . . .

Activities

A. On your own, try this.

1. Think of an animal that might have watched people at play.
2. Think of a way to tell what the animal was and what the people were doing.
3. Think of a problem the animal might have as he tried to play.
4. Plan a story the animal might tell to his friends about his experiences.
5. Write your story. Draw a picture to go with it.

B. Share your story with the class.

11. Writing about a Sport

Read the story below. Then answer the questions.

Skydiving

A sport I would like to try is skydiving. A sky diver falls fast at first. Then his parachute opens and he just floats through the air. He sees cars that look like ants crawling on white ribbons. He sees grassy fields that look like painted floors. Then he lands and everything looks big again.

- What sport did the writer want to try? What sentence tells you this?
- What do sky divers do in their sport? What sentences tell you this?
- What do sky divers see as they float?
- What sentences tell you this?

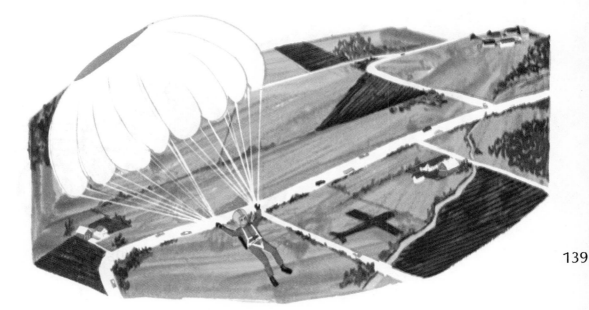

With your classmates, talk about the following sports. What do you know about each sport? How might things look, sound, feel, or smell to a person doing the sport?

Scuba diving

Mountain climbing

Bareback riding

Motorcycle racing

Drag racing

Sailing

Horse racing

Water skiing

Activities

A. Choose a sport you would really like to try. Write a story about the sport you chose.

1. Tell the name of the sport first.

2. Tell what to do in the sport.

3. Tell how you think things would look, or sound, or feel, or smell as you did the sport.

B. Make a picture to go with your story. Show your story and picture to your class.

12. Listening to Poetry

Listen as your teacher reads the following poem to you.

THE BALLOON

I went to the park
And I bought a balloon.
It sailed through the sky
Like a large orange moon.
It bumped and it fluttered
And swam with the clouds.
Small birds flew around it
In high chirping crowds.
It bounced and it balanced
And bowed with the breeze.
It skimmed past the leaves
On the tops of the trees.
And then as the day
Started turning to night
I gave a short jump
And I held the string tight
And home we all sailed
Through the darkening sky,
The orange balloon, the small birds
And I.

—KARLA KUSKIN

Listen as your teacher reads the poem again. Answer these questions.

- What did the speaker do to have fun?

- Would you like to have the speaker as a friend? Why?

For Discussion

Read aloud parts of the poem which answer the following questions.

1. Where did the speaker buy the balloon? What kind of balloon was it?

2. What did the wind make the balloon do? Find lines that tell you.

3. When did the speaker fly the balloon?

4. What thing in the poem could happen only in the land of make-believe?

Activities

A. Draw a picture which shows something that happened in this poem.

B. Show your picture to the class.

CHAPTER 6

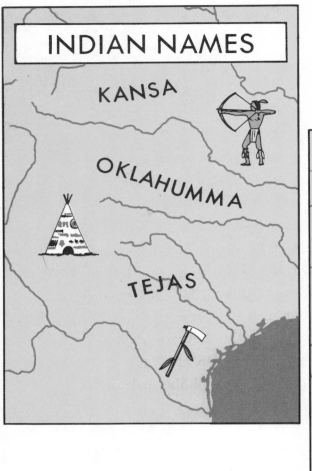

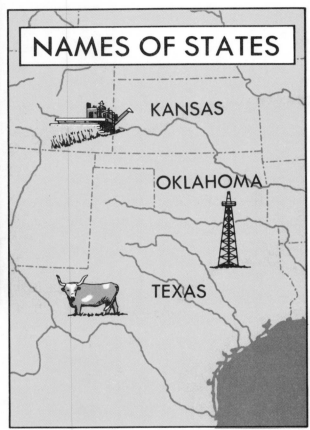

1. Names of States

Read the names of the places shown on both maps softly to yourself. Answer this question.

- ■ Which Indian names and names of states are very much alike?

The early explorers and settlers liked many of the Indian names for places. They borrowed some of these names. In time, the Indian words became words of the English language.

Read the names on both maps again. How were the Indian names changed?

For Discussion

A. Here are some names of states and the Indian names they came from. How were the Indian names changed?

1. Utah—Ute

2. Massachusetts—Massaadchueset

3. Missouri—Emissourita

4. Wisconsin—Wishkonsing

5. Michigan—Mishigamaw

B. Below are some words used by American Indians. Each word became the name of a state. See if you can give each state name.

1. Arizonac	7. Nebrathka
2. Minisota	8. Misisipi
3. Iliniwek	9. Oheo
4. Arkansaw	10. Idaho
5. Alibamu	11. Dakotas (two states)
6. Tanasi	12. Alakshak

147

2. Compound Words That Begin Alike

Look at the examples below. What new word do you make when you add *sun* to *glasses*? To *flower*?

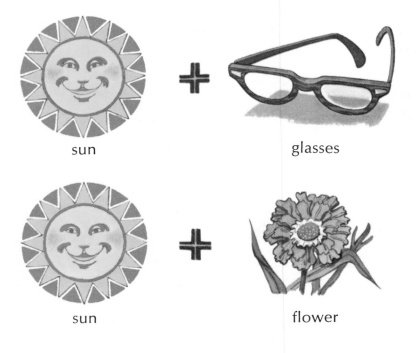

sun

glasses

sun

flower

Words such as *sunglasses* and *sunflower* are made by putting together two separate words. Words made in this way are called **compound words.** What other compound words can you think of that begin with *sun?*

For
Discussion

148   Tell what two words were put together to make each of the compound words in group *1* and group *2.* Then see if

you can add one other compound word to the words in each group.

Group 1

waterwheel   watermelon

Group 2

rainbow   raindrops

For Practice

Oral Answer each question below with a compound word. Two of the words in each question will help you think of an answer.

1. What is the time of the day when the sun sets?
2. What is the time of the day when the sun rises?
3. What flower has the color of butter and the shape of a cup?
4. What do you call a box for mail?
5. What kind of house is made to play in?

Written Write ten compound words. Make them by putting together words from group 1 and group 2. Use only one of the words of group 2 in each compound word.

Group 1	Group 2	
1. air	1. plane	road
2. bed	2. plant	room
3. milk	3. weed	mile
4. space	4. ship	book
5. gear	5. shift	scrap
6. tea	6. taxi	cup
7. corn	7. meal	mouse
8. ear	8. ring	floor
9. eye	9. glasses	face
10. finger	10. ear	print

149

3. Compound Words That End Alike

Study the groups of pictures below. Read the words under the first two pictures in each group. What compound word could you write under the third picture of each group?

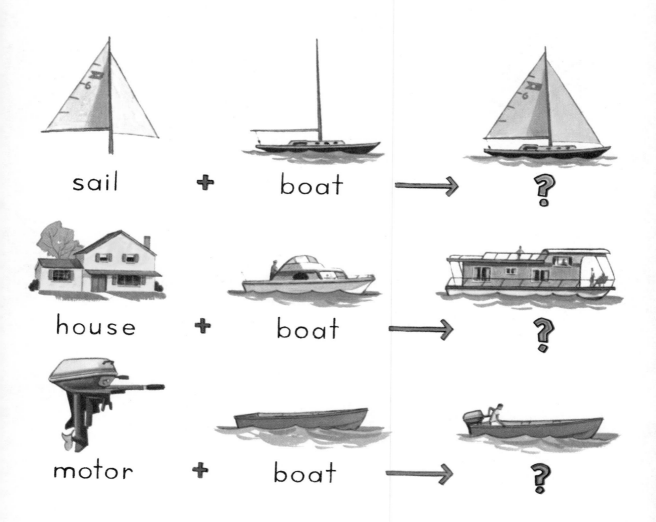

sail + boat → ?

house + boat → ?

motor + boat → ?

■ Which part of the word is the same in every compound word you made?

Knowing the meaning of one word in a compound word often helps you know what the compound word means. What compound word ending with *boat* can you think of besides *sailboat, houseboat,* and *motorboat?* What does the compound word mean?

For Discussion

What compound words that end with *fly, fish,* or *ball* can you make from each group of words below?

1. base	**2.** house	**3.** gold
foot	butter	sun
snow	dragon	sail
soft	horse	cat

For Practice

Written Write ten compound words. Make them by putting together words from group *1* and group *2*. Use each word in group *2* twice.

Group 1		Group 2
1. base	**6.** basket	**1.** light
2. moon	**7.** rain	**2.** man
3. milk	**8.** musk	**3.** ball
4. water	**9.** over	**4.** coat
5. day	**10.** post	**5.** melon

ON YOUR OWN

Try to make up a few new compound words of your own. For example, you might call a man who flies jets a jetman. Give your words to a friend. See if he can tell what they mean.

4. Noun Determiners

Study the following sentences. Each word in color is a noun. What word comes before each noun?

The apple is good.	The apples are good.
A peach is good.	These peaches are good.
An orange is good.	Those oranges are good.
That pear is good.	Two pears are good.
This carrot is good.	Three carrots are good.
One melon is good.	Four melons are good.

Each of the words before a noun is a **noun determiner.** Read the sentences in each group again. All the nouns in the first group are singular nouns. All the nouns in the second group are plural nouns.

- Which noun determiners go with singular nouns? Which go with plural nouns?

- Which noun determiner is in both groups?

Think about noun determiners. Do they come before or after nouns? What are some noun determiners?

What noun would you use to go with each picture below? Is the noun singular or plural? Which noun determiners could you use with each noun? Why?

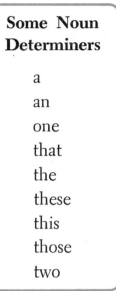

Some Noun Determiners

a

an

one

that

the

these

this

those

two

For More Practice
See Page 324

For Practice

Oral Read each of these sentences. Use a noun determiner in each sentence.

1. — shoe is small.
2. — bee stung me.
3. — rabbits jumped out.
4. — elephant is big.
5. — grapes are ripe.
6. — monkey fell.
7. — boys are big.
8. — pencil is sharp.
9. — balloon broke.
10. — girls ran fast.

153

5. Nouns in the Subject Part

Read the sentences below. The part that is in color is the subject part.

1. **The kitten** feels soft.

2. **A puppy** feels soft.

3. **An otter** feels soft.

4. **Snowflakes** feel soft.

Look at the words in the subject part of each sentence above.

■ Does every subject part have a noun?

■ Which subject parts have a noun determiner?

■ Which subject part has no noun determiner?

Think about what you have learned about the subject part of a sentence.

■ What two kinds of words make up the subject part of some sentences?

■ What kind of word can be used by itself as the subject part of some sentences?

The subject part of each sentence below is in italics. Which subject parts are made with both determiners and nouns? Which subject part is made with just a noun?

1. *A street* is torn up.
2. *The streets* are torn up.
3. *The child* is laughing.
4. *Children* are laughing.

For Practice

Written A. Add a subject part to each predicate given below. Use a determiner and a noun in each sentence.

1. — broke.
2. — has a shell.
3. — ate the bait.
4. — were red and yellow.
5. — had a sharp point.

For More Practice
See Page 324

6. — wore heavy shoes.
7. — had green leaves.

B. Make up four sentences of your own. Use one of these nouns without a determiner in the subject part of each sentence.

1. children
2. birds
3. cups
4. shoes

155

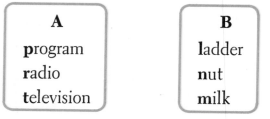

6. Alphabetical Order

Say the alphabet. The names of the letters shown above are in **alphabetical order.**

Now say the names of the letters in each group below. Which groups of letters are in alphabetical order? How can you tell?

a b c d e   f h m s u   p q r t s

Now look at the lists of words below.

A	B
program	**l**adder
radio	**n**ut
television	**m**ilk

- Which list of words is in alphabetical order? How can you tell?

- How could you change the other list to put the words in alphabetical order?

156

A. How would you put each group of letters below in alphabetical order?

1. a b c d f e   4. a c b d e f

2. a b c f d e   5. h k i l j m

3. a b d c e f   6. p r q s y z

B. How would you put each list of words below in alphabetical order?

1	2	3
apples	beef	rice
oranges	pork	oats
bananas	mutton	corn
plums	lamb	wheat

For Practice

For More Practice
See Page 324

Oral How would you put the words in each list below in alphabetical order?

1	2	3
dinner	cousin	goose
breakfast	aunt	chicken
lunch	uncle	duck

Written Write the words in each list in alphabetical order.

1
onion
carrot
beet

2
spider
grasshopper
ant
worm

3
stem
trunk
branch

4
stone
rock
pebble
clay

157

7. More about Alphabetical Order

about

acorn

add

aerial

Look at each word above. Answer these questions.

- What is the first letter?
- What is the second letter?
- In what order are the second letters?

Are the words in alphabetical order? Which letters in each word do you have to look at before you can tell?

Now look at each of these words.

bank

bench

bowl

birthday

- What is the first letter?
- What is the second letter?
- Is the list in alphabetical order? Which letters in each word do you have to look at before you can tell?
- How can you change the list to put the words in alphabetical order?

158

Which lists of words below are in alphabetical order? How did you decide?

1	**2**	**3**
camp	factory	wagon
cent	frozen	window
chalk	firefly	wolf
cotton	floor	write

For
Practice

For More Practice
See Page 325

Written Decide which letters to look at to put each list below in alphabetical order. Write the words in each list in alphabetical order.

1	**2**	**3**	**4**
button	dandelion	frozen	mosquito
blanket	diamond	funny	measure
board	dust	factory	minute
broom	drum	finger	mouse

ON YOUR OWN

Think of three words beginning with each letter below. Write the words. Ask a friend to put the words in alphabetical order.

1. n   **3.** k

2. s   **4.** w

8. For Review

Read and discuss the questions below.

A. Which words below are compound words? How can you tell? What other compound words can you name?

1. rainbow
2. sunlight
3. baseball
4. firefly
5. snowman
6. softly

B. What noun would you use to name each picture? What noun determiners could you use with each noun?

Some Noun Determiners

a	this	one
an	that	two
the	these	three
	those	four

C. The subject part of each sentence below is in italics. Which subjects are made with both noun determiners and nouns? Which subjects are made with nouns alone?

1. *This clock* is slow.
2. *Caramels* taste sweet.
3. *Baseball* is exciting.
4. *The dog* barked at me.

D. Which list of names below is in alphabetical order? How did you decide? How would you put the other two lists in alphabetical order?

1. Maria
   Carl
   Hugh

2. Daniel
   Dennis
   Douglas

3. Michelle
   Marian
   Melissa

160

Read the directions for each exercise below. Follow the directions, writing your answers on your own paper.

A. Write the word in each pair below that is a compound word.

1. football, basket
2. fruit, blackberry
3. teacup, plate

4. milkman, house
5. sailboat, lake
6. overcoat, clothes

B. Add a subject to each of the sentences below. Use a different noun determiner and noun each time.

7. — is on the table.
8. — was lost.
9. — built a birdhouse.
10. — drew a picture.

C. Write the names in each group below in alphabetical order.

11.	12.	13.
Howard	Susan	Alice
Maureen	Sally	Arlene
Linda	Sidney	Amy
Peggy	Sonja	Ann

161

10. Talking about Things to Ride

Listen as your teacher reads the following poem aloud.

THE KAYAK

Over the briny wave I go,
In spite of the weather, in spite of the snow:
What cares the hardy Eskimo?
In my little skiff, with paddle and lance,
I glide where the foaming billows dance.

Round me the sea-birds slip and soar;
Like me, they love the ocean's roar.
Sometimes a floating iceberg gleams
Above me with its melting streams;
Sometimes a rushing wave will fall
Down on my skiff and cover it all.

But what care I for a wave's attack?
With my paddle I right my little kayak,
And then its weight I speedily trim,
And over the water away I skim.

Now read the poem by yourself. Answer these questions about it.

- Who is the speaker in the poem?

- What is he riding in?

- What makes the ride fun?

- Would you like a kayak ride? Why?

For Discussion

See how many things to ride your class can name. These questions may help you think of things to name.

1. What can you ride in on land?

2. What can you ride in on water?

3. What can you ride in through the air?

Activities

A. Find or draw a picture of something you want to ride in someday.

B. Show your picture to someone. Tell him about it. Answer these questions.

1. What makes the thing move? Muscles? Wind? Gasoline engine? Electric motor? Gravity?

2. Who runs the thing?

3. Who rides in it?

4. What are some good things about it? What are some bad things?

11. Writing a Riddle

Read the following riddle. At what point are you sure of the answer?

I am a little shorter than my nine-year-old owner. I have a flat top made of boards. I have two runners. My owner lies on me when he rides. Together we slide down snow-covered hills in winter. What am I?

Now read the riddle again. Answer these questions.

- In which sentence do you learn the size of the thing?

- In which sentences do you learn how it looks?

- What does it move forward on?

- How is it used?

- When is it used? Where?

For Discussion

Suppose a minibike could make up a riddle about itself. What might it say? Answering these questions may help you decide.

1. What might the minibike say about its size?
2. What might it say about what makes it go?
3. What might it say about its sounds and smells?
4. What other clues might it give to help someone know what it is?

A. Think of something to ride. Make up a riddle about the thing. In your riddle, make believe that the thing is the speaker. Here are some things it might tell.

1. Its size
2. Its shape
3. How it moves forward
4. How it smells and how it sounds
5. Who uses it and when they use it

B. Form groups of four or five boys and girls. Take turns reading and guessing the riddles you have written.

C. Talk about the riddles. Decide which were the best ones. Decide why they were the best.

12. Playing a Role

Read what the saleslady and the mother are saying. They are in the doorway of the mother's home. They are living in the year 2000.

SALESLADY: Good morning. I'm your jet-shoe saleslady. May I come in?

MOTHER: You're what? Say, what's holding you a foot above the floor?

SALESLADY: I'm glad you asked. I'm wearing jet shoes. They're our latest invention. I'd like to sell you a pair. They'll cut your work in half.

MOTHER: I'd like that. Do come in. Tell me about the shoes. Will they fit me? How do they work? How much are they?

Make believe that you can listen to the two people.

- What answers might the salesperson give to the mother?

- What words might the salesperson use to tell about the shoes?

- What might the mother say?

For Discussion

Suppose you wanted to make up a play for two persons living in the year 2000. One person could be selling

something to ride in or on. The other person could be the buyer.

1. What could the salesperson sell? A car that flies? A jet-powered bicycle? A rocket-powered boat?

2. What name could the thing have?

3. What words could the salesperson use in telling about it?

4. What questions could the buyer ask?

5. What answers could the salesperson give?

Activities

Make up a play for a salesperson and a mother or father to act out.

13. Choosing Words to Show Feelings

The lists of words below are from two stories about the elephant. How do you feel about the elephant after reading each list?

A
dirty-gray color
ear-splitting call
squinty eyes
clumsy feet
awful smell

B
slate-gray color
high-pitched call
half-closed eyes
broad feet
peanut smell

- Which words are the same in both lists?

- Which words tell about color? About sound? About smell?

A. Suppose that you like old cars such as the one in the picture. What words could you use to tell about these things?

1. Its color
2. Its shape
3. How it sounds
4. How it smells

B. Suppose that you dislike old cars such as the one in the picture. What words could you use to tell about these things?

1. Its color
2. Its shape
3. How it sounds
4. How it smells

Activities

A. Make a picture of something you can ride. It could be a school bus, a car, a truck, or something else.

B. Make a list of words that you could use in telling how you feel about the thing you drew. Use words that tell about these things.

1. Its color
2. Its shape
3. How it sounds
4. How it smells

C. Show your picture and list to a friend. Have him guess your feelings about the thing you drew.

169

14. Listening to Poetry

Listen as your teacher reads the following poem aloud.

AN EASY DECISION

I had finished my dinner
Gone for a walk
It was fine
Out and I started whistling

It wasn't long before

I met a
Man and his wife riding on
A pony with seven
Kids running along beside them

I said hello and

Went on
Pretty soon I met another
Couple
This time with nineteen
Kids and all of them
Riding on
A big smiling hippopotamus

I invited them home

—KENNETH PATCHEN

Listen as your teacher reads the poem to you again. Then answer the following questions.

- Is the writer telling about a real walk or a make-believe walk?

- Is the name of this poem a good one for the poem? Why?

For Discussion

A. Read aloud the parts of the poem which answer each of the questions below.

1. Was the writer happy or sad when he began his walk?

2. What was unusual about the first group described? About the next group?

3. What did the writer do when he met the second group?

B. Why do you think the writer liked the second group better than the first group?

Activities

Form groups of four or five boys and girls. Plan a way to use pictures to show the story the poem tells. Then do these things.

1. Each person may draw one picture.

2. Put the pictures on a bulletin board. Be sure to place them in the right order to tell the story.

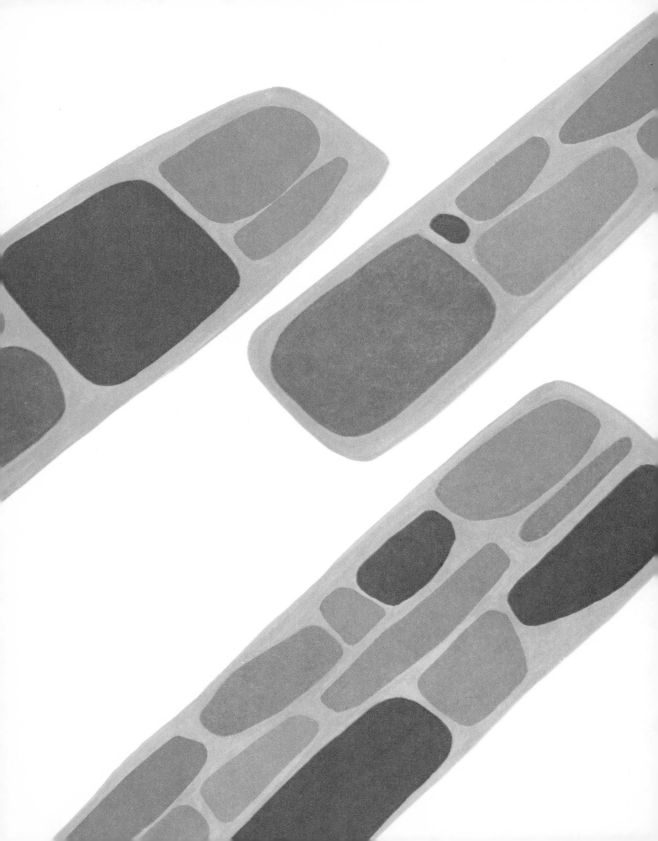

CHAPTER 7

1. Words That Name Animal Sounds

ARK
ARK

G·R·R·R·R

YIP·YIP

Look at the dog in each picture. Then answer these questions.

- What sound does each dog make?
- Which word—*growl, yelp,* or *bark* —names the sound made by the old dog? By the mean dog? By the puppy?

People have made up many words that name sounds made by animals. What gave them the ideas for the words?

For Discussion

What word is used to name a sound that each of these animals makes?

duck

snake

cat

sheep

cow

ON YOUR OWN

See if you can make up a sound that the animal shown here might have made. Then make up a word of your own to name the sound. Say your word to a friend. See if he can guess the sound that you made up for the animal.

175

2. Words with Prefixes

Look at the examples below. What new word do you make when you add *re* to *build?* To *pay?* To *open?*

re **+** build → —

re **+** pay → —

re **+** open → —

Many new words are made by adding a word part like *re* to the beginning of a word. This word part is called a **prefix.**

Each word below has a prefix printed in heavy type.

untrue   **pre**soak   **dis**obey

■ What prefixes were used?

Think about the prefixes *re*, *un*, *pre*, and *dis*. Do they come at the beginning or at the end of a word?

For More Practice See Page 325

For Discussion

What prefix and word were joined to make each word in italics below? What other words can you think of that begin with *un*? With *re*? With *pre*? With *dis*?

1. un + afraid → *unafraid*

2. re + open → *reopen*

3. pre + cook → *precook*

4. re + load → *reload*

5. dis + like → *dislike*

6. dis + agree → *disagree*

For Practice

Oral Make words by adding *re*, *un*, *pre*, or *dis* to each word below.

1. *re*—heat, play, write

2. *un*—happy, kind, wrap

3. *pre*—school, judge, war

4. *dis*—connect, agree, trust

Written Join each prefix and word below. Write the new words.

1. un + lawful
2. re + make
3. pre + pay
4. dis + approve
5. un + button
6. dis + honest
7. re + do
8. dis + appear
9. pre + view
10. re + join

177

3. Words with Suffixes

Look at the examples below. What new word do you make when you add *ish* to *boy?* To *girl?* To *kitten?*

boy **+** ish → —

girl **+** ish → —

kitten **+** ish → —

Many new words are made by adding a word part like *ish* to the end of a word. The word part is called a **suffix.** Two other common suffixes are *ly* and *er.*

Think about the suffix *ish.* Does a suffix come at the beginning or at the end of a word?

What word and suffix were joined to make each word in italics below? What other words can you think of that end with the suffix *ly?* With the suffix *er?*

1. friend **+** ly → *friendly*

2. slow **+** ly → *slowly*

3. smooth **+** ly → *smoothly*

4. bowl **+** er → *bowler*

5. camp **+** er → *camper*

6. climb **+** er → *climber*

**For
Practice**

For More Practice
See Page 325

Oral Read each pair of sentences below. Tell the word and the suffix that were joined to make each word in italics.

1. John's father builds houses.
   He is a *builder.*

2. The woman acts like a mother.
   The woman is *motherly.*

3. Inez will buy something.
   Inez will be the *buyer.*

4. Joe felt a little like a fool.
   Joe felt *foolish.*

5. Miss Johnson talked very loud.
   She talked *loudly.*

6. Betty likes to lead people.
   She is a good *leader.*

Written Join each word and suffix below. Write the new words.

1. father + ly

2. fever + ish

3. start + er

4. brother + ly

5. like + ly

6. child + ish

7. finish + er

8. self + ish

9. fight + er

10. friend + ly

179

4. Proper Nouns

Look at the picture above. Find the name of the girl, the boat, and the lake.

- Which of the names has one word? Two words? Three words?

- How do the words in each name begin?

Special names like *Maria*, *Lazy Days*, and *Big Bass Lake* are called **proper nouns.**

Think about what you have learned. How could you describe a proper noun in a few words?

180

A. Which of the following words do you think are proper nouns? How did you decide?

1. river
2. Donald Cosgrove
3. bridge
4. Empire State Building
5. alligator
6. Ohio River
7. Golden Gate Bridge
8. building
9. man
10. Pedro
11. dog
12. girl

B. What proper nouns can you think of that name special persons? Special places? Special things?

**For
Practice**

For More Practice
See Page 326

Oral Read each sentence below. Tell what proper noun is used in each one.

1. I sit next to Inez.
2. Have you seen Lake Michigan?
3. We saw the Smoky Mountains.
4. Our plane flew over Denver.
5. He lives in Sandburg Village.

Written Complete the following sentences by using a proper noun in place of each blank. Write your sentences. Use capital letters to begin each proper noun.

1. My name is —.
2. My street is called —.
3. My school is named —.
4. My teacher's last name is —.
5. I know a pet named —.
6. The name of my state is —.
7. I would like to see the state of —.
8. The tallest building I know is called the —.
9. The park nearest my home is called —.
10. The name of the holiday I like best is —.

181

5. Proper Nouns in the Subject Part

Read the sentences below. The part that is in color is the subject part.

1. **Canada** has good roads.

2. **Michael Rollins** won the race.

3. **Labor Day** is a holiday.

4. **Lake Victoria** is near the equator.

Look at the words in the subject part of each sentence above.

- Does every subject part have a proper noun?

- Do any of the subject parts have a word like *a, an,* or *the?*

Think of what you have learned about the subject part of a sentence. What kind of noun can be used alone as the subject part of some sentences?

For Discussion

Look at each picture below. Then do these things.
1. Use a proper noun to name each thing.
2. Use each proper noun as the subject of a sentence.

For Practice

Oral   Replace each subject in italics in the sentences below with a different proper noun. Read each sentence you make.

1. *New York* is a state.
2. *Sarah* walked to school.
3. *Independence Day* is a holiday.
4. *India* is a country.
5. *Lake Michigan* is a lake.

Written   Use a proper noun as the subject of each of the following

For More Practice
See Page 326

sentences. Write the sentences you make.

1. — talked to me.
2. — is the name of a friend.
3. — gave me gum.
4. — is a street.
5. — is a country.
6. — is our President.
7. — drives a truck.
8. — works in a store.
9. — asked me to come.

183

6. Words in a Picture Dictionary

Look at the part of a picture dictionary page shown below. Notice that the words are in alphabetical order.

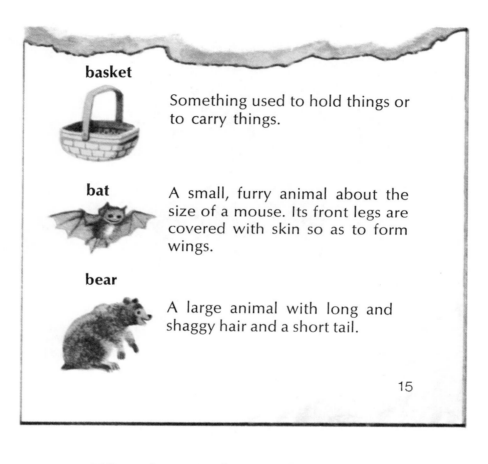

basket

Something used to hold things or to carry things.

bat

A small, furry animal about the size of a mouse. Its front legs are covered with skin so as to form wings.

bear

A large animal with long and shaggy hair and a short tail.

15

- What three words are told about on this page of the dictionary?

- Why does *basket* come before *bat?*

- What does the dictionary say about each word?

A. Which of these make-believe words could you use to name each picture?

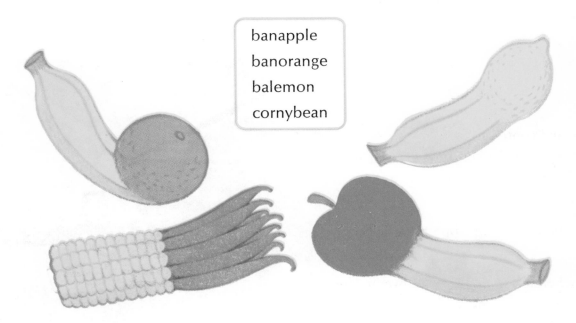

banapple

banorange

balemon

cornybean

B. How would you arrange the words *banapple, banorange, balemon,* and *cornybean* in a dictionary you might make? What might your dictionary say about each word?

For
Practice

A. Make up a word like *autobike* or *gloveshoe* to name something that doesn't really exist. Write the word on a piece of paper. Also write a sentence that tells enough about the thing so that someone could draw it. Ask a friend to draw a picture to go with the word.

B. Make a class picture dictionary of the words your class has made up. Put the words into alphabetical order in your dictionary.

C. See if you can find some words in your dictionary as someone reads them to you.

7. Using a Dictionary

The part of a page shown below is from a dictionary. Read the page and answer the questions below.

helicopter An aircraft that is lifted from the ground and moved by means of propellers on the top.

heliport An airport for helicopters.

helmet A protective covering for the head worn by soldiers and football players.

- What three words does this page from a dictionary tell you about?

- What is the order of the words on the page?

- What does the dictionary tell you about a heliport? About a helmet?

All dictionaries make statements telling what words mean. Do you think that you could use a dictionary to find the meaning of *helmsman?* What would you do?

For Discussion

What meaning does the dictionary you use give for each word below? What sentences can you make to show that you know what each word means?

1. mantel   **3.** kelp

2. cockle   **4.** winch

For Practice

Written   Use a dictionary to find what each word in italics below means. Then write your answer to each question.

1. Is a *hedgehog* a furry animal?

2. Can you wear a *dory?*

3. Does a *jellyfish* have fins?

4. Is a *hart* bigger than a horse?

5. Does your state have a *firth?*

8. For Review

Read and discuss the questions below.

A. Which word in each group below has a prefix? How can you tell? What are some other words with prefixes?

1	2	3
play	kind	view
replay	unkind	preview
player	kindly	viewer

B. Which word in each group below has a suffix? How can you tell? What are some other words with suffixes?

1	2	3
make	like	build
remake	dislike	rebuild
maker	likely	builder

C. Which word in each group below is a proper noun? How did you decide? What are some other proper nouns?

1	2	3
boy	city	lake
Robert Brown	San Diego	Lake Erie

D. What are some proper nouns that you can use as the subject part of each sentence below?

1. — is my friend.
2. — is the name of a city.
3. — is the name of a lake.

Read the directions for each exercise below. Follow the directions, writing your answers on your own paper.

A. Write the word in each pair below that contains a prefix.

1. untrue, true   3. player, replay

2. wrapper, rewrap   4. prejudge, judge

B. Write the word in each pair below that contains a suffix.

5. roughly, rough   7. impolite, politely

6. rework, worker   8. honestly, dishonest

C. Write the word in each pair below that is a proper noun.

9. girl, Teresa   11. Bill Martin, boy

10. Denver, city   12. lake, Lake Michigan

D. Write each sentence below. Complete each sentence with a proper noun.

13. — is the name of a city.

14. — is the name of a boy I know.

15. — is the name of a girl I know.

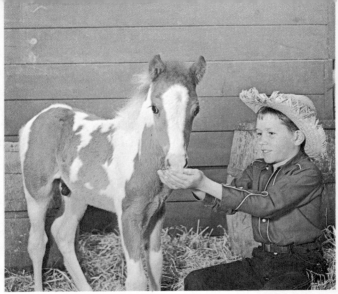

Dwight Ellefsen   H. Armstrong Roberts

10. Talking about Pets

Look at each animal in the pictures. Then answer these questions.

- Would you really want one of the pets? Why or why not?

- Would you like some other pet better than any shown in the pictures? If so, why?

For Discussion

A. Make believe that you can have one of the pets. Then answer these questions.

1. Which pet would you choose? Why?

2. Could you keep the pet where you live? Why?

3. What would you have to do to take care of your pet?

B. None of the animals in the picture have a name. What
name would you give each animal? Why?

Activities

A. Choose someone to work with. Make a list of animals that you would like to have as pets. Then make up and write a name for each of the pets.

B. If you already have a pet of your own, you may want to do these things.

1. Think of a time when your pet got in trouble or got you in trouble.
2. Draw a picture to show what happened.
3. Write a title for your picture.
4. Show your picture to someone. Tell him what happened.

C. If you don't have a pet but would like one, you may want to do these things.

1. Think of an animal you would like most as a pet.
2. Draw a picture of the animal. Give him a name. Write the name on your picture.
3. Show your picture to someone if you wish to. Tell why you chose the name. Also tell why you would like the animal.

11. Making Up a Riddle

Listen as your teacher reads the following riddle. See if you can give the answer.

My name is Satin. I am soft and white, and I have pink ears, pink eyes, and a pink nose. What I like best is eating carrots and lettuce. What am I?

Were you able to guess the answer? Why?

Go back and read the riddle again. Think about what you can do to make up a riddle. Answering these questions will help you know what to do.

- What does the first sentence tell about the pet? What hint does the name give to let you know how the pet feels when you touch him?

- What does the second sentence tell about the pet? What word tells how the animal really feels to the touch? What words tell how it looks?

- What hint does the third sentence give?

Suppose that you were going to write a riddle about the pet in the picture.

1. What might be a good name to use for the pet? Why?

2. What words might you use to tell how the pet feels when you hold it?

3. What words could you use to tell how the pet looks?

4. What might you say to tell what the pet likes best?

Activities

A. Write a riddle about a pet you would like. Here are some things you might tell in your riddle.

1. In the first sentence, tell the name of the pet.

2. In the second sentence, tell how the animal feels. Also tell how it looks.

3. In the third sentence, tell what the animal likes to do best.

B. Your class may want to form groups for listening to riddles. Each person in a group may read his riddle. The others may try to guess the answer.

C. Talk about the riddles in each group. Decide which riddles were the best and why they were the best.

12. Playing a Role

Have you ever read this poem before?

Look what we found
in the park
in the dark.
We will take him home.
We will call him Clark.

He will live at our house.
He will grow and grow.
Will our mother like this?
We don't know.

—DR. SEUSS

Read the poem again. This time make believe that you are one of the people who found the pet. Answer these questions which you might be asking yourself at the time.

- Will my mother let me keep Clark as a pet?
- What will I say to my mother?

The poem is a good one to use in making up a play. Could your class make up the play? What could you do to help?

Suppose your class does make up a play. Here are some questions that may help you plan.

A. Where could we give our play? What characters do we need?

B. How would you act if you were one of the children?

1. Would you be excited when you first walked into the house with Clark? Or would you be sheepish?

2. What would you say to your parents?

C. How would you act if you were one of the parents?

1. Would you laugh when the children walked into the house with Clark? Would you be angry? Would you be frightened? Would you faint?

2. What would you say to your children?

Activities

Form groups of four or five children each. Each group can put on a play telling what happened when the children in the poem arrived home with Clark.

Here are some suggestions for each group to follow.

1. Before you begin acting, draw and color a large picture of Clark for use in the play.

2. Act out the play four or five times, with each pupil taking a different part each time. After each performance, discuss how you might make the play better.

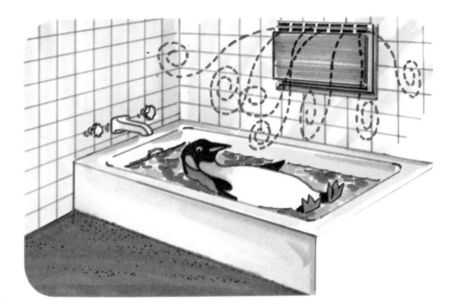

13. Writing a Letter for Fun

Read the following letter which a girl wrote just for fun. What did she know about penguins?

Dear Animal Catcher,

I've always wanted a pet penguin. Would you catch one for me?

I could keep it in the bathroom. I'd put an air-conditioner in there to keep the room cold, and I'd keep the tub full of water so it could swim.

I really would take good care of my penguin.

With love,
Anita

Suppose you wanted to write some just-for-fun letters to an animal catcher for a zoo.

1. What kind of pet would you ask him to catch for you? A flamingo? A hippopotamus? A whale? What about a fire-breathing dragon?

2. What could you do to find out the kind of care your pet would need?

3. What could you say in your letter to show that you would take good care of the pet?

Activities

A. Write a just-for-fun letter to an animal catcher for a zoo. Ask him to catch you an unusual pet.

B. Choose someone to work with. Ask him to read your letter as you read his. Read the letter for fun. Then check the letter for spelling, capital letters, and periods. Each letter writer may then copy his letter.

C. Find or make a picture that shows the pet you ask for.

D. You may have fun showing your picture and reading your letter to the class. The class may decide whether or not the animal catcher should send you the pet that you asked for.

14. Listening to Poetry

Listen as your teacher reads the following poem to you.

MISSING

Has anybody seen my mouse?

I opened his box for half a minute,
Just to make sure he was really in it,
And while I was looking, he jumped outside!
I tried to catch him, I tried, I tried. . . .
I think he's somewhere about the house.
Has *anyone* seen my mouse?

Uncle John, have you seen my mouse?

Just a small sort of mouse, a dear little brown one,
He came from the country, he wasn't a town one,
So he'll feel all lonely in a London street;
Why, what could he possibly find to eat?

He must be somewhere. I'll ask Aunt Rose:
Have *you* seen a mouse with a woffelly nose?
Oh, somewhere about—
He's just got out. . . .

Hasn't *anybody* seen my mouse?

—A. A. MILNE

Listen as your teacher reads the poem again. As you listen, think about the answers to these questions.

Why might someone want a mouse for a pet?

What might be some bad things about having a pet mouse?

Where would you look for a lost pet mouse?

For Discussion

Read aloud parts of the poem which help answer the following questions.

1. How did the mouse get away? What lines in the poem tell you this?

2. How did the mouse look? What lines tell you?

3. What lines in the poem tell why the owner of the pet was worried?

Activities

A. Draw a picture to show the mouse getting out of its box.

B. Find another poem about a pet.

1. Draw a picture to go with the poem.

2. Practice saying the poem.

3. Show the picture as you say the poem aloud to a friend or to the class.

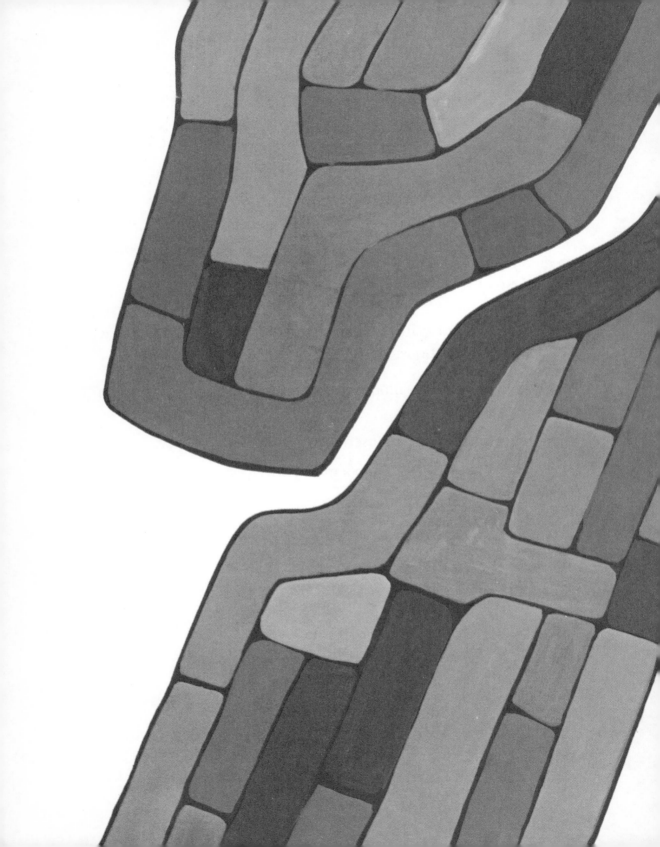

CHAPTER 8

1. Words That Describe Noises

Listen as your teacher reads the poem aloud.

GALOSHES

Susie's galoshes
Make splishes and sploshes
And slooshes and sloshes,
As Susie steps slowly
Along in the slush.

They stamp and they tramp
On the ice and concrete,
They get stuck in the muck and the mud;
But Susie likes much best to hear

The slippery slush
As it slooshes and sloshes,
And splishes and sploshes,
All round her galoshes!

—Rhoda W. Bacmeister

■ What words describe the noises that the galoshes make in the slush?

■ What gave the poet the idea for such words as *splishes* and *sploshes*?

Have you ever made up words that describe sounds? If so, what are they?

For Discussion

Which word in the box best describes a noise made by each thing shown below? What other words can you think of to describe the sounds?

squeak

zoom

pop

ON YOUR OWN

Listen for words that seem to describe noises. Help make a class list of these words.

2. Adding a Prefix and a Suffix

Look at the examples below. What new words were made by adding both a prefix and a suffix to each word in color?

Prefix			Suffix			
un	+	skill	+	ful	→	unskillful
un	+	friend	+	ly	→	unfriendly
un	+	break	+	able	→	unbreakable

Look at each of the new words again. Then answer these questions.

- What prefix comes at the beginning?
- What suffix comes at the end?

Suppose that you wanted to make up a word by adding the prefix *re* and the suffix *able* to *new*. What would you do? What word would you make?

For Discussion

What prefix and suffix were added to make each word in italics below?

1. turn → *returnable*
2. agree → *disagreeable*
3. brother → *unbrotherly*
4. success → *unsuccessful*

204

Oral Make new words by joining the prefix, suffix, and word in each example below.

1. un, ly — happy

2. un, ful — health

3. un, ly — man

4. un, ly — clear

5. re, able — place

6. re, able — turn

7. dis, ful — taste

8. dis, ful — trust

9. un, ness — kind

10. un, ness — tidy

Written Join the prefix, word, and suffix in each example below. Write each new word you make.

1. un + common + ly

2. un + equal + ly

3. un + like + ly

4. un + kind + ly

5. re + heat + able

6. re + mark + able

7. re + build + able

8. un + sink + able

9. un + skill + ful

10. un + truth + ful

205

3. Adding Two Suffixes

Look at the first example. What word can you make by joining the word *cheer* with the suffixes *ful* and *ness?*

Now look at the second example. What word can you make by joining the word *cheer* with the suffixes *less* and *ly?*

cheer **+** ful **+** ness

cheer **+** less **+** ly

Think about the two words you have just made.

- What suffixes are at the end of each word?

What word can you make by adding the suffixes *less* and *ness* to the word *cheer?* What word can you make by adding two suffixes to *hope?*

For Discussion

What suffixes were added to make each word in italics?

1. care	→	*carelessness*
2. joy	→	*joyfully*
3. sheep	→	*sheepishly*
4. thought	→	*thoughtfulness*
5. pain	→	*painlessly*

For More Practice
See Page 327

Oral Read the following groups of sentences. Which word and suffix or suffixes were used to make each word in italics?

1. John always told the truth.
   He was *truthful*.
   He answered *truthfully*.

2. Pedro walked with care.
   He was *careful*.
   He carried the little bird *carefully*.

3. Ann could not sleep.
   She was *sleepless*.
   She did not know the cause of her *sleeplessness*.

4. Laura was filled with joy.
   She was *joyful*.
   Her *joyfulness* pleased her father.

5. Barbara showed great glee.
   She was *gleeful*.
   Her *gleefulness* made everyone happy.

Written Join each word with the suffixes in each example below. Write the words you make.

1. sleep + less + ness
2. care + less + ly
3. care + less + ness
4. truth + ful + ness
5. color + ful + ly

ON YOUR OWN

Think of five words that are made by joining two suffixes with a word. Use the words to make some cards like these.

Work with a friend. See how many words the two of you can make by using the cards.

207

4. Personal Pronouns

Read the poem softly to yourself. Then answer the questions below it.

FIGHT

Cat and I
We had a fight;
I hit,
Cat bit,
We quit.

—Jean Jaszi

- Who is doing the talking?

- What word did she use in talking about herself? About herself and the cat?

The words *I* and *we* are **personal pronouns.**

Here are some other personal pronouns. Which of these personal pronouns would you use in a sentence about yourself?

me	you	her	us
he	it	they	
she	him	them	

For Discussion

Which of the personal pronouns above would you use in sentences about each of the following?

1. A girl
2. A boy
3. An aunt
4. An uncle
5. A girl and a boy together
6. Yourself and others

For Practice

For More Practice
See Page 327

Oral Read each pair of sentences below. What personal pronoun would you use in place of the words in ( ) in each sentence?

1. (A boy) was hit by the ball.
   The ball hit (a boy).
2. (A girl) called the nurse.
   The nurse heard (the girl).
3. (Two persons) were scared by the noise.
   The noise scared (the persons).
4. (Joe and Al) won the game.
   The prize goes to (Joe and Al).

Written Complete each sentence below with one of these personal pronouns. Write your sentences.

   it   you   us   we   me

1. Did — see the car?
2. — was very old.
3. The car came toward Ann and —.
4. — shouted at the driver.
5. The car missed —.

5. Personal Pronouns as the Subject Part

Read each sentence below. The part that is in color is the subject part.

1. **We** like the ice-cream man.

2. **He** knows all of us.

3. **I** like to hear his truck.

4. **It** makes wonderful sounds.

5. **You** would like the truck.

6. **She** likes the truck.

7. **They** like the truck, too.

Look at the word in the subject part of each sentence above.

■ Is each subject part a personal pronoun?

Think about what you have learned. What personal pronouns can you use as the subjects of sentences?

Use each of these personal pronouns—*he, she,* or *it*—as the subject part of a sentence. The picture will help you think of ideas for your sentences.

For
Practice

For More Practice
See Page 327

Oral Read each sentence. Then read it again. This time use *he, she,* or *it* in place of each subject part in italics.

1. A *fireman* drove the truck.

2. An *orange* costs less than a pineapple.

3. *The nail* was bent.

4. *The man* sells candy.

5. *My sister* weighs eighty pounds.

Written Complete each sentence below, using one of the following personal pronouns. Be sure to use each personal pronoun one time.

we   she   he   it   I   you

1. — is Fred Mason.
2. — heard a funny noise.
3. — are going to a show.
4. — has a new dress.
5. — made a loud bang.
6. — should see my new shoes.

211

6. Guide Words

Look at the page from a dictionary. *Beach* is the first word listed on the page. The last word listed is *beaver*. Where else do the words *beach* and *beaver* appear on the page?

The words at the top of a dictionary page are called **guide words**. Is this a good name for them? Why?

The next example shows guide words from a different dictionary.

nylon   450   **oatmeal**

- What is the first word you could look up on page 450? What is the last word?

Think of what you have learned about guide words. How can they help you find words in a dictionary?

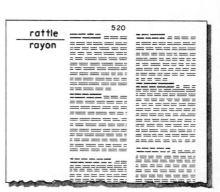

A. What are the guide words in the example? Which of the words below might you find on page 520? Why?

1. raw   3. record

2. raven   4. rascal

B. What are the guide words in the example below? Which words below the example could you find on page 404? Why?

     reward   404   **ridge**

1. rhubarb   3. rib   5. rice

2. rhea   4. ridge   6. rind

Oral Look at the pairs of guide words below. Tell two words that you might find on a page having these guide words.

1. absent — birth

2. change — dare

3. fair — grab

4. its — main

5. visit — zone

Written Find the following page numbers in a dictionary. Write the guide words you find on each page.

1. page 50

2. page 100

3. page 150

4. page 200

5. page 250

213

7. Finding Meanings

Read the sentence below. Do you know what it means? If not, why not?

He rolled a hogshead on the floor.

Now read what one dictionary says about *hogshead*.

hogs head (hogz′hed), **1** a large barrel containing from 100 to 140 gallons. **2** a liquid measure equal to 63 gallons.*

■ How many meanings does *hogshead* have? How can you tell?

■ What is each meaning?

Read the example sentence again. What does *hogshead* mean in the sentence? How do you know?

For Discussion

hose (hōz), **1** a tube of rubber or something else that will bend, for carrying any liquid for short distances. See the picture. A hose used in pumping gasoline into automobiles. **2** stockings. **3** long, tight breeches worn by men in olden times.*

Read what the dictionary says about *hose*. Then answer these questions.

1. How many meanings are given?

2. Which meaning goes with the picture?

3. Which meaning fits the word in italics in each of the sentences below?

She bought a pair of *hose*.

She bought a piece of garden *hose*.

For Practice

cane (kān), **1** a slender stick used as an aid in walking. **2** beat with a cane. **3** a long, jointed stem. The stems of sugar cane and bamboo are canes. **4** any of various plants having such stems, such as sugar cane. **caned, can ing.***

Oral Study the meaning of *cane*. Then tell which meaning fits the word in italics in each sentence below.

1. The schoolmaster *caned* the boy.

2. The man walked with a *cane*.

3. The farmer harvested *cane*.

4. She sucked juice from the *cane*.

Written A. Write the number of the meaning that fits the word in italics in each sentence below.

horse hair (hôrs′hār′), **1** hair from the mane or tail of a horse. **2** made of horsehair; stuffed with horsehair.*

1. She sat in a *horsehair* chair.

2. He bought *horsehair* from a farmer.

B. Write the number of the meaning that fits the word in italics in each sentence below.

hop per (hop′ər), **1** person or thing that hops. **2** a grasshopper or other hopping insect. **3** container to hold something and feed it into another part. A hopper is usually larger at the top than at the bottom. See the picture.*

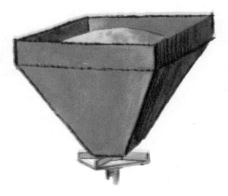

1. The boy used a *hopper* for bait.

2. The man filled the *hopper* with wheat.

215

8. For Review

Read and discuss the questions below.

A. What is a prefix? A suffix? Which words below have both a prefix and a suffix? Which end with two suffixes?

1	2
returnable	thoughtfulness
unfriendly	carelessly

B. Which of the following words are personal pronouns? What other personal pronouns can you name?

1. he   **3.** house   **5.** boy   **7.** she

2. they   **4.** you   **6.** we   **8.** it

C. What are some personal pronouns that you could use as the subject of each sentence below?

1. — was found.   **3.** — isn't very old.

2. — were frightened.   **4.** — won the game.

D. Which words below would you expect to find on a dictionary page with the guide words *hello* and *hurry?* Why?

1. horse   **3.** hat   **5.** home

2. hunt   **4.** hen   **6.** hit

E. Which meaning of *foot* fits each word in italics? What are some other words with more than one meaning?

1. The path was only a *foot* wide.

2. We walked to the *foot* of the hill.

3. He limped along on one *foot.*

foot (fùt), **1** the part of the leg that a person stands on. **2** the bottom part of something. **3** twelve inches.

216

Read the directions for each exercise below. Follow the directions, writing your answers on your own paper.

A. Write the word in each pair below that has both a prefix and a suffix.

    1. truthfully   **2.** remarkable

        untruthful   clearly

B. Write the word in each pair below that ends with two suffixes.

    3. painlessly   **4.** unkindly

        unskillful   carefulness

C. Write these sentences. Use a different personal pronoun as the subject of each.

    5. — went home.   **7.** — were not here.

    6. — is on the team.   **8.** — isn't open yet.

D. Write the word in each pair that you would expect to find on the dictionary page in the picture.

    9. fox, frugal

   10. fern, frame

E. Which meaning of *cleaner* fits each sentence below? For each sentence, write the meaning that fits that sentence.

clean er (klēn′ər), **1** a worker whose duty it is to keep things clean. **2** something used to help remove dirt or stains.

    11. We used a new *cleaner* on the rug.

    12. The *cleaners* did a good job.

10. Talking about Wild Animals

Read the following poem softly to yourself.

FURRY BEAR

If I were a bear,
  And a big bear too,
I shouldn't much care
  If it froze or snew;
I shouldn't much mind
  If it snowed or friz—
I'd be all fur-lined
  With a coat like his!

For I'd have fur boots and a brown fur wrap,
And brown fur knickers and a big fur cap.
I'd have a fur muffle-ruff to cover my jaws,
And brown fur mittens on my big brown paws.
With a big brown furry-down up to my head,
I'd sleep all the winter in a big fur bed.

—A. A. MILNE

Now read the poem again. Did the poet think it might be fun to be a bear in winter? Why?

What kinds of wild animals do you know? Which kind of wild animal would you like to be for a little while? Why?

For Discussion

A. What is the first wild animal you think of when you hear each word below?

1. spotted
2. smelly
3. striped
4. creepy

5. prickly
6. strong
7. tiny
8. fierce

B. Answer these questions.

1. What animals have fur? Hard shells? Wings?
2. What kind of wild animal do you like best?
3. What can your favorite wild animal do that you think is fun?

11. Collecting Sayings about Animals

Busy as a bumblebee in a bucket of tar

More fun than a barrel of monkeys

As lacking in privacy as a goldfish

■ What animal is named in each saying above?

People use sayings like these again and again. Which of the sayings have you heard? What does each of the sayings mean?

Read each saying below. What does each saying mean?

1. Merry as a cricket
2. Nervous as a long-tailed cat in a roomful of rocking chairs
3. Happy as a bear on a honey farm
4. Clumsy as an elephant in a roomful of eggs
5. Worried as a turkey in November

Activities

A. Using some of the following ways, collect sayings about animals.

1. Ask people to tell you a saying they know.
2. Listen for sayings as you watch television.
3. Look for sayings in stories.

B. Form groups of four or five boys and girls each. Listen to the sayings each person has collected. Talk about ways to use each saying in a sentence.

C. Draw a picture for one saying you like.

1. Write your saying on your picture.
2. Show your picture to the class.

12. Collecting Superstitions about Animals

Read the conversation below. It takes place between two friends walking along a path.

SARAH: Stop, Lodi. Don't move.
LODI: What's wrong?
SARAH: That toad. It's crossing our path. Now we'll have bad luck. And for a whole year!
LODI: How foolish can you be! That toad can't change our luck.

- How was the toad supposed to change luck?

- Does Sarah's belief about toads make sense? Why?

The belief that actions of animals can change luck is a **superstition.** Do you think superstitions are true? Why?

A. What superstition have you heard about each animal shown below? Do any of the superstitions make sense? Why?

B. What other superstitions about animals have you heard?

A. Ask grown-ups to tell you some superstitions about animals, or use a superstition you heard in class. Then do these things.

1. Draw a picture of the animal.
2. Write the superstition under the picture.
3. Show your picture to the class.

B. Form groups of three or more boys and girls.

1. Choose a superstition about an animal to act out.
2. Plan a way to act out the superstition.
3. Act out your play for the class.

13. Naming and Describing

Look at the picture of a make-believe animal.

- What parts come from a frog?
- What parts come from a pigeon?
- How did the animal get its name?

FRIGEON

Read the description of the make-believe animal. What does it tell about the size, shape, color, and sounds of a frigeon?

A frigeon can fit nicely into an empty, round oatmeal box. His head and the underside of his body are shiny green with large black spots. Blue and peach feathers cover his body and wings. A cheery sound of *knee-deep, knee-deep* fills the air each time the frigeon sings.

A. What name might you give to each animal shown in the pictures? Explain your answers.

B. What words could you use to describe the size, shape, color, and sounds of each make-believe animal above?

Activities

A. Divide into groups of three or four children. Each person may wish to make a model or a large picture of a make-believe animal. Working together, give each animal a name. Put the models or pictures on a table.

B. Write a description of the make-believe animal you like best, but don't give its name. Give your description to a friend. See if he can find the animal that you described.

225

14. Listening to Poetry

Listen as your teacher reads the following poem to you.

THE REASON FOR THE PELICAN

The reason for the pelican
Is difficult to see:
His beak is clearly larger
Than there's any need to be.

It's not to bail a boat with—
He doesn't own a boat.
Yet everywhere he takes himself
He has that beak to tote.

It's not to keep his wife in—
His wife has got one, too.
It's not a scoop for eating soup.
It's not an extra shoe.

It isn't quite for anything.
And yet you realize
It's really quite a splendid beak
In quite a splendid size.

—JOHN CIARDI

Listen as your teacher reads the poem again. Be ready to answer these questions.

- Would you like to see a pelican? Why?

- Did the poet think that the large beak was any good at all? What makes you think so?

For Discussion

What lines from the poem answer each question below?

1. Is a pelican's beak too large or too small?

2. How did the poet know that the beak was not to bail a boat with? Was not to keep a wife in?

3. Is the beak a scoop? A shoe?

4. What did the poet realize as he looked at the pelican's beak?

Activities

Draw a picture which shows a pelican trying to use his beak in an unusual way. Show your picture to the class.

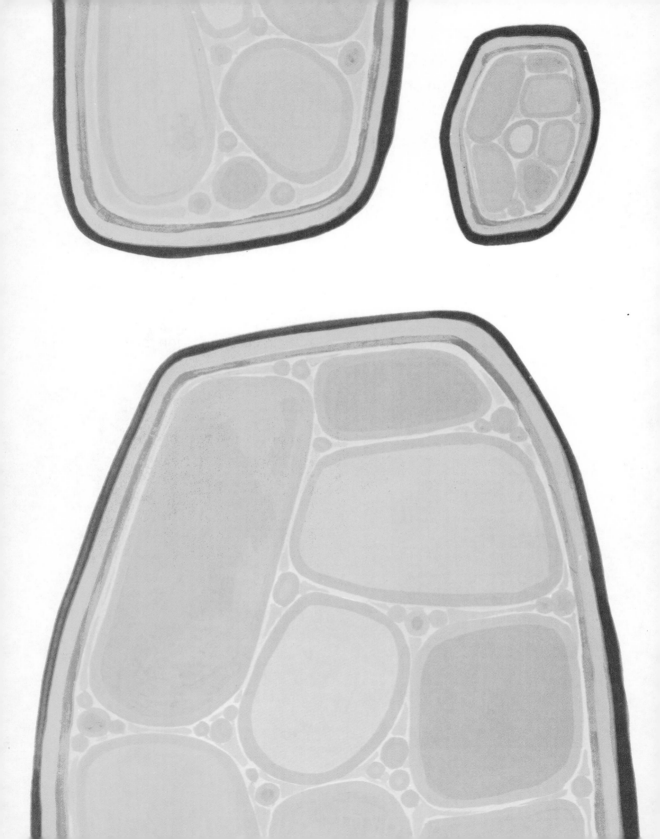

CHAPTER 9

1. Games with Words

Read each name. Then spell each name first forward and then backward.

Now read each word above. Then spell each word first forward and then backward.

- What are some other words like *Otto*, *Anna*, and *Bob?*

- What are some other words like *pan*, *tub*, and *trap?*

For Discussion

A. What words do you know that are spelled the same way forward and backward? HINT: Adding letters to these word frames will help you think of words.

1. p — p	**4.** g — g
2. b — b	**5.** d — d
3. e — e	**6.** H — nnah

B. What words do you know that form other words when they are spelled backward? HINT: These word frames will help you think of words.

1. po — l	**4.** t — r
2. p — t	**5.** n — w
3. t — n	**6.** n — p

2. The Prefix *un*

Read both sentences below. Notice that they have the same meaning.

    1. The lion is **not friendly.**

    2. The lion is unfriendly.

Compare the sentences, answering these questions about them.

- What words are the same?

- What word in sentence 2 takes the place of the two words in color in sentence *1?*

- What meaning does the prefix *un* add to *friendly?*

For
Discussion

What word below each pair of pictures begins with the prefix *un?* What meaning does *un* add to each word?

safe

unsafe

For
Practice

Oral Read each pair of sentences below. What meaning does *un* add to each word in italics?

1. The bill was not paid.

   The bill was *unpaid.*

2. His address was not known.

   His address was *unknown.*

3. The glass was not breakable.

   The glass was *unbreakable.*

4. His story was not believable.

   His story was *unbelievable.*

5. The tiger was not caged.

   The tiger was *uncaged.*

happy

unhappy

233

3. More about the Prefix *un*

Read the sign. Notice that one thing is done at night. The opposite thing is done in the morning.

Look at the words *cover* and *uncover*.

- Which word has the prefix *un?*

- Does the prefix *un* mean "not"? Or does it mean "do the opposite of"?

Think about what you have learned about the prefix *un.* What are two different meanings that the prefix *un* can add to a word?

Read each pair of sentences below. What meaning does *un* add to each word in italics?

1. I tie my shoelaces each morning.

I *untie* my shoelaces each night.

2. He will load the truck at the farm.

He will *unload* the truck in town.

3. The baby was not happy.

The baby was *unhappy*.

Written Each word in the list that follows begins with the prefix *un*. Decide what meaning *un* adds to each word. Then write a sentence using each word.

1. unbutton

2. uncage

3. unpack

4. undo

5. unfold

6. unknown

7. unable

8. unwind

4. Verbs

The subject part of each sentence below is in color. Read the sentences. Then answer the questions.

The diesels pull longer trains now.

My best friend pulled two carrots.

Mary Jo writes well today.

Mary Jo wrote poorly yesterday.

The days seem better now.

The room seems very quiet.

- What is the predicate part of each of the sentences?

- What is the first word in each predicate part?

The first word in the predicate part of each sentence above is called a **verb.** What verb do you see in each sentence?

For Discussion

The subject of each sentence below is in italics. What is the predicate? What is the verb? How can you tell?

1. *The firemen* climb ladders now.
2. *The firemen* climbed ladders yesterday.
3. *Chocolate cakes* smell very good.
4. *The chocolate cake* smells very good.
5. *My little brother* eats too much candy.
6. *The boy* ate too much candy.

236

For More Practice
See Page 328

Oral Complete each sentence below with as many different verbs as you can.

1. My friend — a question.
2. The man — a candy bar.
3. A red truck — down the street.
4. The family — a new house.
5. My toothache — much better now.

Written Write each sentence below. Circle each verb. HINT: The subject of each sentence is in italics.

1. *White snow* covered the ground.
2. *My brother* drank the milk.
3. *Balloons* drift with the breeze.
4. *The little pony* is frisky.
5. *The clouds* seem darker now.
6. *The painters* painted the room.
7. *Lemons* taste sour.
8. *The ice cubes* melted fast.
9. *The pilot* made a mistake.
10. *Everyone* makes mistakes.

ON YOUR OWN

Draw a picture that makes you think of a subject for a sentence. Write the subject. Ask someone to add different predicates to your subject. Try picking out each verb he uses.

237

5. Two Verb Forms

Each sentence below has a plural subject shown in color. What is the verb?

> **Sentences with Plural Subjects**
>
> The lemons taste sour.
>
> The cookies taste sweet.
>
> The potato chips taste salty.

Each sentence in the next group has a singular subject. What ending does each verb have?

> **Sentences with Singular Subjects**
>
> The lemon tastes sour.
>
> The cookie tastes sweet.
>
> The potato chip tastes salty.

Verbs have two forms to use with certain singular and plural subjects. One verb form ends with s. The other form has no s.

Study the two groups of sentences again.

- Which verb form is used with a singular subject like *the lemon?*
- Which verb form is used with a plural subject like *the lemons?*

Which form of the verb in ( ) would you use to complete each sentence below? Why?

1. Some old cars — funny. (look, looks)

2. My brother — fast. (walk, walks)

3. The dog — at the moon. (bark, barks)

For More Practice
See Page 328

Written   A.   Write each sentence below, using a singular subject in place of each subject in italics. Make the needed changes in the verb.

1. *The apples* taste good.
2. *The marbles* look small.
3. *The dogs* chase after cars.
4. *The horns* make a noise.
5. *The small ice cubes* melt fast.

B. Write each sentence below, using a plural subject in place of each subject in italics. Make the needed changes in the verb.

1. *The black cat* howls at night.
2. *The candle* shines brightly.
3. *The boy* skates well.
4. *The girl* sings songs.
5. *The car* rides very well.

239

6. Writing Contractions

Compare the sentences in cartoon *1* with the sentences in cartoon 2. Then answer these questions.

- Which sentences have the same words?
- Which sentences have different words?
- How are *is not* and *isn't* different?

The mark between the *n* and *t* of *isn't* is called an **apostrophe.** It shows where a letter was left out. What was the letter?

Isn't is a short way of writing two words as one word. *Isn't* is a **contraction.** What other contractions do you know?

For Discussion

A. How does a contraction differ from the words it replaces?

B. Which of the following are contractions? How can you tell? What two words does each contraction replace?

1. do not
2. hasn't
3. had not
4. has not
5. hadn't
6. don't
7. aren't
8. shouldn't
9. didn't

For Practice

For More Practice
See Page 329

Written   Write each sentence that follows. Use a contraction in place of the words in italics.

1. The cookies *were not* baked.
2. You *must not* run on the deck.
3. Mary *was not* sick.
4. It *does not* look like rain.
5. We *are not* going.
6. My aunt *could not* come.
7. Our friends *are not* here.
8. Those boys *were not* hungry.
9. This *is not* my best day.
10. He *did not* go home.

7. More about Writing Contractions

Read the sentences below. Compare the words in color.

You will catch cold.

You'll catch cold.

- What is the contraction?
- What letters of *you will* are left out of *you'll?*
- What does the apostrophe show?

Here are some more words and contractions. What letter or letters does each apostrophe replace?

you are	→ you're	they will	→ they'll
let us	→ let's	we have	→ we've
he is	→ he's	he had	→ he'd
it is	→ it's	she has	→ she's
I am	→ I'm	of the clock	→ o'clock

For Discussion

A. Which of the following are contractions? How can you tell?

1. its   3. they're   5. they've

2. it's   4. there   6. who'll

B. Where should you put the apostrophe in each of the contractions in italics below? Why?

1. he is   → *hes*

2. you have → *youve*

3. I am   → *Im*

4. you are → *youre*

For Practice

For More Practice
See Page 329

Written Write each sentence that follows. Use a contraction in place of the words in italics.

1. *I will* do it myself.

2. *It will* be too late.

3. *She is* a good friend.

4. *You had* better go.

5. *She had* gone there before.

6. *Everyone is* going.

7. *He is* on third base.

8. *They are* winning the game.

9. *It is* almost six o'clock.

10. *We are* leaving now.

ON YOUR OWN

Make a collection of contractions that sound like other words. Write the groups of words like this.

he'll—heal—heel

they're—there—their

8. For Review

Read and discuss the questions below.

A. What two meanings can the prefix *un* add to a word? Use the examples below in explaining your answer.

1	**2**
Tom is *not happy*.	We *load* the car at home.
Tom is *unhappy*.	We *unload* the car at Grandmother's.

B. The subject of each sentence below is in italics. What is the predicate of each sentence? What is the verb? How can you tell?

1. *Our team* won the game.

2. *Mother* baked a big cake.

3. *We* built a birdhouse.

C. With which kind of subject would you use a verb form that ends in *s*—a singular or a plural subject? Use the examples below in explaining your answer.

1	**2**
The cookie *tastes* good.	The cookies *taste* good.
That skate *looks* rusty.	Those skates *look* rusty.

D. Which group of words below contains contractions? How did you decide? How would you make contractions of the other group of words?

1	**2**
isn't	do not
didn't	has not
you'll	they will

244

Read the directions for each exercise below. Follow the directions, writing your answers on your own paper.

A. For each word below, write **not** or **do the opposite of** to show the meaning that the prefix *un* adds to that word.

1. untie
2. unpleasant
3. unbreakable
4. uncover

B. The subject of each sentence is in italics. Pick out the verb for each sentence. Write the verbs.

5. *Dwight* wrote a thank-you note.
6. *The pilot* made a perfect landing.
7. *Brown leaves* covered the ground.
8. *My brother* skates very well.

C. Write these sentences. Complete each with a form of the verb in ( ).

9. Sally (like, likes) her new dress.
10. Those oranges (taste, tastes) sour.
11. The sky (looks, look) very dark this morning.
12. A bus (leave, leaves) every ten minutes.

D. Write the contraction of each pair of words below. Remember to use an apostrophe in each contraction.

13. could not
14. they are
15. you have
16. are not

10. Talking about Cartoon Characters

Look at the cartoon pictures on the next page.

- What is the name of each cartoon character?

- What is each of these characters like?

- What other cartoon characters are often shown with each cartoon character? What are they like?

Who is your favorite cartoon character? Why do you like this character?

A. Make a class cartoon display by doing the following things.

1. Have each person in your class bring two or three of his favorite cartoons to class. These can be cut out of newspapers or comic books.

2. As a class, arrange the cartoons on a large poster or on a large roll of paper.

3. Paste the cartoons in place as soon as they are arranged on the poster or on the paper.

B. Mount the class cartoon display on a wall or on a bulletin board.

"THIS ISN'T NO WRONG NUMBER! WE BEEN USING IT FOR *YEARS!*"

11. Making a Cartoon

Look at the cartoon below. Read what is written under the cartoon.

"He wouldn't be so bad if he didn't snore!"

Could you make up another "Marmaduke" cartoon? Study the cartoon again. Then answer these questions.

- Who is Marmaduke? Who are the others in Marmaduke's family?
- What is funny or strange about Marmaduke?

What cartoons might you draw showing Marmaduke at the following places? What words might go with each cartoon?

1. At a neighbor's small swimming pool

2. In a supermarket

3. In a living room listening to music

Activities

A. With a partner, plan and draw two new Marmaduke cartoons. Write words under each cartoon. Put your cartoons on a bulletin board.

B. Make up your own cartoon character. Draw a cartoon showing your character doing something funny. Write words under your cartoon. Display the cartoon.

12. Acting Out a Story

Read the comic strip on the next page.

- How do Charlie Brown and Schroeder play "Train"? What actions do they perform?

- How does Patty stop the game? What does she do?

- What does Charlie Brown do to show his feelings?

For Discussion

Suppose that Charlie Brown was playing each of the following games. Talk about how you might act out the story of what would happen.

1. Building a sand castle with Schroeder

2. Playing checkers with Linus

3. Making a snowman by himself while Snoopy watches

Activities

A. Form groups of three or four boys and girls in each group. Plan to act out a story by doing the following things.

1. Think of a game that Charlie Brown and one or two other "Peanuts" might enjoy playing. Talk about how you might act out the beginning of the game.

2. Talk about how you might act out each thing that would happen.

3. Practice acting out the story your group talks about.

B. Act out your Peanuts story for the rest of the class.

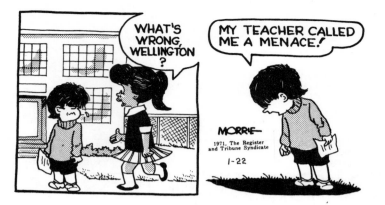

13. Writing a Comic Strip

Look at the comic strip above. Read the words that go with it.

- How is the comic strip divided into parts?

- What is each part about?

- Are words said in each part?

- How do you know who is talking?

Suppose that you were going to draw a "Wee Pals" comic strip in which Wellington says that his grades will go up in upper grade school. Talk about the following.

1. How many parts might be in the comic strip? How
might you show this?

252

2. What might happen in each part?

3. What might be said in each part? How could you show who was speaking?

Activities

A. Make up your own comic strip. Do these things.

1. Think of two or three characters.

2. Think of what your characters are like. Also think of names for them.

3. Now think of something funny that your characters could do or say in a comic strip.

4. Draw your comic strip. Be sure that each part is separate. Also be sure that it is clear who is speaking.

B. Put your comic strip on a bulletin board along with comic strips that your classmates have drawn. Make the bulletin board look like a large "funnies" page in a newspaper.

253

14. Listening to Poetry

Listen as your teacher reads the following poem to you.

SNEEZE

There's a
sort of a
tickle
the size of a
nickel,
a bit like the
prickle
of sweet-sour
pickle;

it's a
quivery
shiver
the shape of a
sliver,
like eels in a
river;

a kind of a
wiggle
that starts as a
jiggle
and joggles
its way to a
tease,

which I
cannot
suppress
any longer,
I guess,
so pardon me,
please,
while I
sneeze.

—MAXINE W. KUMIN

Listen as your teacher reads the poem again. Be ready to answer these questions.

- How did the sneeze begin?

- Why didn't the poet stop the sneeze?

- How was the sneeze like one of your sneezes?

For Discussion

A. What was the size of the sneeze when it began? How did it feel? Read the lines of the poem that tell you these things.

B. How did the poet describe the shape of the sneeze? Read the lines that she used to do this.

C. What happened when the poet could no longer stop the sneeze? Read the lines that tell you this.

Activities

A. Draw a picture to go with the poem.

B. Practice reading the poem aloud. Try to say it all in one breath, except the very end. See if you get a feeling something like a sneeze.

C. Read the poem aloud to someone and show him your picture.

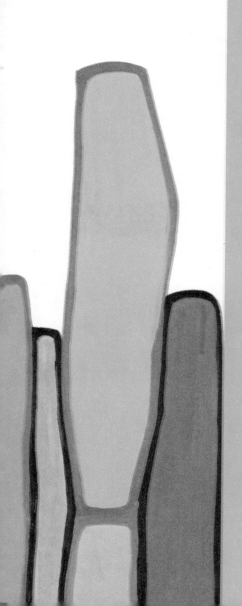

CHAPTER 10

257

1. Words That Repeat Sounds

dingdong

tutu

bowwow

Say each word above in two parts. Answer these questions about the two parts of each word.

- In which word are both parts the same?

- In which word do the parts rhyme?

- In which word do the parts end with the sound *ng* stands for?

Think about each of the words. What is one unusual thing about each word?

What is unusual about each word below?

1. singsong
2. so-so
3. hodgepodge
4. hubbub
5. Ping-Pong
6. rickrack

7. willy-nilly
8. tom-tom
9. tip-top
10. teepee
11. tutti-frutti
12. hobnob

ON YOUR OWN

Make a collection of words that repeat sounds or that seem unusual in some way. Put your words in a list. Show your list to a friend. See if he can tell why you chose each word in your collection.

2. The Suffix *er*

Read the sentences below. Then answer the questions.

A

The man bowls every day.

The man is a good bowler.

B

A squirrel climbs trees very well.

A squirrel is a good climber.

- What suffix was added to *bowl* to make *bowler?*
- What suffix was added to *climb* to make *climber?*

A bowler is a person that bowls. What is a climber? What meaning does *er* add to *bowl?* To *climb?*

What suffix was added to a word to make each word in italics? What meaning did the suffix add to the word?

1. teach   *teacher*   3. play   *player*

2. hunt   *hunter*   4. buy   *buyer*

Oral   A. Change each sentence below. Make the sentences like the second sentence in the example by changing the word in italics.

EXAMPLE:

The man *mines* coal.

He is a miner.

1. My sister *sings* in a choir.

2. The carpenter *builds* houses.

3. My brother *walks* a lot.

4. He *listens* carefully at school.

5. That salesman *works* hard.

B. Change each sentence below. Make it like the second sentence in the example by changing the word in italics.

EXAMPLE:

The man is a good *rider*.

He rides racehorses.

1. The man is a *baker*.

2. The girl is a loud *talker*.

3. The man is a fine *leader*.

4. My father is a *farmer*.

5. His father is a *painter*.

ON YOUR OWN

In some words, like *tiger*, the *er* is not a suffix. See if you can find other words that end in *er* when it isn't a suffix. Make a list of the words you find.

3. One Meaning of *ful*

Read these sentences. Answer the questions below them.

A

Agnes had enough juice to fill a glass.

Agnes had a glassful.

B

Ray had enough berries to fill a basket.

Ray had a basketful.

- What suffix was added to *glass* to make *glassful?*
- What suffix was added to *basket* to make *basketful?*

A glassful of water is enough water to fill a glass. A basketful of berries is enough berries to fill a basket. What meaning does *ful* add to *glass?* To *basket?*

For Discussion

Find the word in each pair of sentences that ends with the suffix *ful*. What meaning does *ful* add to the word?

1. They had enough guests to fill their *house.*
   They had a houseful.

2. John had enough salt to fill the *jar.*
   John had a jarful.

For Practice

Written   Complete the second sentence of each of the following pairs of sentences. Use a word that ends with *ful*. Then write both sentences of each pair.

1. Mary has enough ink to fill a *bottle*.

   Mary has a —.

2. Mother has enough flowers to fill the *vase*.

   Mother has a —.

3. I have enough sliced bananas to fill a *dish*.

   I have a —.

4. Pedro had enough birds to fill a *cage*.

   Pedro had a —.

5. The farmer had enough oranges to fill a *truck*.

   The farmer had a —.

ON YOUR OWN

Think of some words that end with *ful*. Write the words. Put a check mark next to each word in which *ful* means "enough to fill a —."

263

4. A Verb Form That Goes with *Yesterday*

The sentences below each have a different form of the same verb. Compare the three sentences. Then answer the questions below them.

1. The hinges squeak now.

2. The hinge squeaks now.

3. The hinge squeaked yesterday.

- What three forms of *squeak* do you see?

- What ending does *squeak* have in the sentence with *yesterday?*

All verbs have different forms to use in different sentences. Most verbs have a form that ends with *ed*. The *ed* form is used in sentences that tell about something that has already happened.

- Does *squeak* have a form that ends with *ed?*

- What are some other verbs that have a form that ends with *ed?*

For Discussion

The verb in each sentence below is in italics. Read each sentence. Then change *now* to *yesterday*, and read the sentence again. Tell how the form of the verb changes.

1. The girls *skip* rope now.   **2.**   The brakes *squeak* now.

For More Practice
See Page 329

Oral Read the first sentence in each pair. Complete the second sentence with a different form of the verb in italics.

1. The boys *work* now.

   The boys — yesterday.

2. The girls *boil* water now.

   The girls — water yesterday.

3. The men *bowled* yesterday.

   The men — now.

4. Bells *clanged* yesterday.

   Bells — now.

5. The pupils *laugh* now.

   The pupils — yesterday.

Written Complete each pair of sentences below. Use a different form of the same verb in both of the sentences. Use these verbs: *bake, nibble, open, park, rattle.*

1. Bakers — bread now.

   Bakers — bread yesterday.

2. Mice — cheese now.

   Mice — cheese yesterday.

3. Keys — locks now.

   Keys — locks yesterday.

4. Cars — here now.

   Cars — here yesterday.

5. The windows — now.

   The windows — yesterday.

265

5. More Verb Forms

The verb in each sentence below is in color. Compare the sentences in each group. Find out how the verbs differ in form.

A

The rooms feel cold now.

The room feels cold now.

The room felt cold yesterday.

B

The cats eat food now.

The cat eats food now.

The cat ate food yesterday.

- What three different forms of *feel* do you see?

- Which form is used in the sentence with *yesterday?*

- What three different forms of *eat* do you see?

- Which form is used in the sentence with *yesterday?*

Most verbs have a form that ends in *ed* to use in sentences that tell about something that happened in the past. How are verbs like *feel* and *eat* different from most verbs?

How would using *yesterday* in place of *now* change each verb in italics?

1. I *see* a truck there now.
2. I *take* vitamins now.
3. The water *runs* fast now.

For Practice

For More Practice
See Page 330

Oral Change *now* to *yesterday* in each sentence below. Then change the form of the verb in italics. Say each sentence that you make.

1. I *know* the answer now.
2. I *write* small now.
3. The boys *catch* fish now.
4. We *sing* good songs now.
5. They *bring* their lunches now.

Written Make new sentences by changing the *now* in each sentence below to *yesterday*. Then change the form of the verb. Write each sentence that you make.

1. John *throws* rocks now.
2. Geese *fly* high now.
3. I *know* the answer now.
4. Ann *drinks* milk now.
5. Mr. Amos *speaks* softly now.

267

6. Writing Words That Show Ownership

The word in color in the sentence below each picture shows ownership. How do you say each word in color? How do you spell each of the words?

This is **Lodi's** bracelet.

This is a **dog's** toy.

Now study each example below. Answer the questions.

Lodi **+** 's → Lodi's

dog **+** 's → dog's

- What mark and letter were added to *Lodi* to make *Lodi's?* To *dog* to make *dog's?*

- Is the apostrophe used before or after each *s?*

Suppose that you wanted to make a word like *fireman* show ownership. What would you do?

A. What mark and letter were added to a word to make each word in italics show ownership?

1. boy → *boy's*
2. camel → *camel's*
3. cousin → *cousin's*
4. pilot → *pilot's*
5. pirate → *pirate's*
6. monkey → *monkey's*

B. Which word in each example below shows ownership? How can you tell?

1. the seal's fur
2. a lion's roar
3. one lady's dresses
4. a rabbit's foot

**For
Practice**

For More Practice
See Page 330

Written **A.** Change these words to words that show ownership. Write each new word you make.

1. ant
2. baby
3. clown
4. bee
5. mouse
6. crocodile
7. sparrow
8. turkey
9. turtle
10. family

B. Change each example below. Make each word in italics show ownership. Write each new example you make.

1. the tongue of the *dragon*
2. the haircut of the *boy*
3. the head of the *flea*
4. the coat of the *scarecrow*
5. the wings of the *fly*

269

7. More about Words That Show Ownership

Read the two sentences below. The words in color show ownership. Do those words sound alike? Are they exactly alike?

See the **skunk's** cage.　　　See the **skunks'** cage.

- What was added to *skunk* to make *skunk's?*
- What was added to *skunks* to make *skunks'?*

Both *skunk's* and *skunks'* show ownership. Which shows ownership by one skunk? By more than one skunk?

Suppose that you wanted to make a word like *lion* show ownership. What would you do? Suppose that you wanted to make *lions* show ownership. What would you do?

What mark was used with a word ending in *s* to make each word in italics show ownership?

1. scouts → *scouts'*   4. boys → *boys'*

2. nurses → *nurses'*   5. bakers → *bakers'*

3. donkeys → *donkeys'*   6. goats → *goats'*

For Practice

For More Practice See Page 330

Written   A. Change each of these words to a word that shows ownership by adding an apostrophe. Write each new word you make.

1. bears	6. mothers
2. bumblebees	7. ducks
3. caterpillars	8. horses
4. chipmunks	9. lambs
5. cowboys	10. worms

B. Make up one sentence for each example below. Add an apostrophe to each word in italics to make it show ownership.

1. Those *dogs* dog food

2. Three *brides* dresses

3. Two *neighbors* houses

4. Those *dentists* offices

5. These *birds* nests

ON YOUR OWN

Make believe that you gave a present to each of the following.

one sailor   one baby   two clowns

Write sentences using the name of each owner and the present you gave him.

271

Read and discuss the questions below.

A. What word in each sentence below ends with the suffix *er?* What does each word with *er* mean?

1. A person who dreams is a dreamer.

2. A person who sings is a singer.

B. What word in each pair of sentences ends with the suffix *ful?* What does each word with *ful* mean?

1. Mr. Davis borrowed enough tobacco to fill a pipe.
Mr. Davis borrowed a pipeful of tobacco.

2. I bought enough doughnuts to fill a bag.
I bought a bagful of doughnuts.

C. The verb in each sentence below is in italics. Suppose that you change the *every day* in each sentence to *yesterday*. How do you have to change each verb in group *1?* In group *2?*

1	**2**
I *deliver* mail every day.	I *take* vitamins every day.
We *play* games every day.	We *go* to school every day.
They *work* hard every day.	They *see* Peter every day.

D. How would you change each word in ( ) in group *1* to make it show ownership? How would you change each word in ( ) in group *2?*

1. one (girl) hat
one (boy) hat

2. two (girls) hats
two (boys) hats

Read the directions for each exercise below. Follow the directions, writing your answers on your own paper.

A. Write the second sentence in each pair. Complete it with a word that ends with the suffix *er*.

1. Mr. James teaches music.
   He is a music —.

2. John Lepes likes to go hunting for bear.
   He is a bear —.

B. Write the second sentence in each pair. Complete it with a word that ends with the suffix *ful*.

3. We bought enough furniture to fill a room.
   We bought a — of furniture.

4. I have enough nickels to fill a pocket.
   I have a — of nickels.

C. Rewrite each sentence, changing *every day* to *yesterday*. Be sure to change the form of each verb.

5. I polish my shoes every day.
6. We visit our grandmother every day.
7. My parents drive to work every day.
8. My brothers wear hats every day.

D. Find the word in each sentence that shows ownership. Write it on your paper.

9. Where did you see my father's car?
10. Where are the teachers' cars?

273

10. Talking about Vacations

Look at the pictures on the next page.

- What is the name of the place in each picture?

- Have you ever visited any of the places in the pictures? If so, which places?

- Which of these places would you like to visit? Why?

A. What places in the United States have you enjoyed visiting? What did you enjoy about these places?

B. If you could go anywhere in the United States for a vacation, where would you like to go? Why?

Make a class vacation display. Here are some of the kinds of things you can do to make the display.

1. Bring to class pictures, postcards, snapshots, and souvenirs of interesting vacation places.

2. Draw pictures of vacation places you would like to visit. Put the name of the vacation place on each picture.

3. Draw pictures of things that you like to do on a vacation. Give each picture a title.

Everglades, Florida

Florida Department of Commerce

H. Armstrong Roberts

New York City

Grant Heilman

Grand Canyon, Arizona

11. Planning a Vacation

Look at the picture below. The picture shows what one girl would pack for her summer vacation if she could go where she would like.

- Where would the girl like to go?

- How would the girl get to the place where she would like to take a vacation?

- What would the weather be like there? How do you know?

- What would she do there?

For Discussion

What plans would you make for vacations in these places?
1. The Sahara Desert
2. The Panama Canal
3. The Himalayan kingdom of Sikkim

Activities

A. Think of an unusual place where you would like to take a vacation. Plan the following things.
1. What to wear
2. How to get there
3. What to take with you to use when you get there

B. Form groups of four or five people in each. Read your vacation plans to the rest of the group, but don't name the place where you are going. Have each person in your group draw a picture of the place that he guesses you are planning to visit.

C. Display the pictures that show the place you chose as a vacation place.

12. Writing a Letter

Heading

August 29, 197—

Greeting

Dear Sharon,

How are you enjoying the hot summer at home? It is winter here, and the temperature is 30 degrees below zero. Luckily, I brought heavy clothing and snowshoes.

Body

This is really a fun vacation. I've made friends with a penguin called Winston. Did you know that penguins once had large wings and could fly? Now they have small wings that they use for swimming.

I'll call you next Tuesday when I come home. There is so much to tell you.

Your friend,
Carol

Closing
Signature

Sender's
Address

Carol Rizzo
Little America Island
Antarctica

Receiver's
Address

Sharon Lieberman
8653 North Catalpa Street
Westchester, Illinois 60153

278

- What are the five parts of the letter?

- Where are commas and capital letters used in the heading, greeting, and closing?

- What is each part of the letter about?

- Where is Carol's address on the envelope?

- Where is Sharon's address?

For Discussion

Pretend that you are answering Carol's letter. Talk about the following things.

1. What might you write about?

2. What might you say in each part of the letter?

Activities

A. Pretend that you are on vacation at an unusual place. Write a letter to a friend telling about your vacation. Address an envelope to go with the letter.

B. Have a friend read the letter and check it to be sure that it has all five parts. Have your friend check the spelling and punctuation, too. Then have him check the envelope.

C. Display your letter.

13. Listening to Poetry

Listen as your teacher reads the following poem aloud.

IN TIME OF SILVER RAIN

In time of silver rain
The earth
Puts forth new life again,
Green grasses grow
And flowers lift their heads,
And over all the plain
The wonder spreads
    Of life,
    Of life,
    Of life!

In time of silver rain
The butterflies
Lift silken wings
To catch a rainbow cry,
And trees put forth
New leaves to sing
In joy beneath the sky,
As down the roadway
Passing boys and girls
Go singing, too,
In time of silver rain
    When spring
    And life
    Are new.

—LANGSTON HUGHES

Listen as your teacher reads the poem again. Then answer these questions.

- What time of year was the poet writing about? How can you tell?
- Did the poet like the time of year he wrote about? What makes you think so?

For Discussion

Suppose that you wanted to make a picture for this poem.

1. What kinds of plants would you show? What lines tell you this?

2. What things would you show in the sky? What people would you show on a roadway? What lines tell you these things?

3. Would the land be hilly or flat? What line helps you decide?

Activities

A. Make a picture for the poem.

B. See if you can find another poem about spring or about rain.

1. Practice reading the poem aloud.

2. Draw a picture for your poem.

3. Show the picture to someone. Also read the poem for him.

For Individual Needs

Composition

282

1. A Model for Stories

When you write a story, you have to decide where to put your name and the date, where to put the title, and where to begin the story. You can use the following story as a model.

Teresa Reilly   October 10, 197–

Blif the Martian

    Blif and Blof were Martians. Blif was telling Blof about his trip to Earth. He told Blof that there were two kinds of people there. One kind had arms and legs, and the other kind had four wheels and a metal body. Blif said that the ones with arms and legs were prettier, but there seemed to be more of the metal kind.

Points to Observe

- ◉ Your name and the date go on the first line.
- ◉ The story title goes in the middle of the third line.
- ◉ The story begins on the fifth line.
- ◉ The first word in each paragraph of a story is indented.

2. How to Write Story Titles

⊙ Some story titles that you make up will have just one or two words. In that case, begin each word with a capital letter.

Bowling   A Surprise

⊙ Other story titles that you make up may have more than two words. Here is how to write this kind of story title.

1. Always begin the first word with a capital letter.

The Haunted House   A Quiet Day

2. Begin important words like *first*, *flight*, *last*, and *birthday* with capital letters.

My First Flight   My Last Birthday

3. Begin short words like *in*, *a*, and *the* with small letters when they come in the middle of the title.

Lost in a Cave   A Horse in the Attic

For Practice

A. Here are some titles for stories. Decide which words in each title should begin with capital letters. Then write the titles on your paper.

1. danger	**5.** the invisible man
2. clipper	**6.** lost in space
3. the secret	**7.** four boys on a raft
4. two friends	**8.** a ride in a balloon

B. Make up two story titles that have at least four words. Write the titles on your paper. Remember to begin the first word and each important word with a capital letter.

3. Grouping Sentences in Paragraphs

Try to read the following story. Is it hard to understand?

Armbruster the Great

Tonight all five thousand of us will sneak up on the grasshopper. My name is Armbruster. This morning a giant of a grasshopper pushed me off a flower petal. We're going to tickle him until he begs us to stop. I'm an ant. I was so angry that I came right home to tell my family.

Now try reading the same story with the sentences arranged in a different order. Is it easier to understand now?

Armbruster the Great

My name is Armbruster. I'm an ant. This morning a giant of a grasshopper pushed me off a flower petal. I was so angry that I came right home to tell my family. Tonight all five thousand of us will sneak up on the grasshopper. We're going to tickle him until he begs us to stop.

Both stories above contain sentences grouped into a paragraph. One of the things that you have to do when you write a story is to group your sentences in paragraphs. But that is not all. You also have to try to arrange your sentences in an order that makes sense. If you do, your stories will be easy to understand.

Points to Observe

Look at the second story again. Notice these things about the paragraph.

⊙ The first word in the paragraph is set in, or indented.

⊙ All the sentences in the paragraph tell about the same idea.

⊙ The sentences in the paragraph are arranged in an order that makes sense.

For Practice

A. Write the sentences in the following story as a paragraph. Be sure to indent the first word in the paragraph.

1. Once there was a bridge painter who became afraid of high places.
2. He stopped working on the highest spots and painted only the walkway.
3. Then he became afraid of that, and he painted only the ramp leading to the bridge.
4. Finally, he gave up bridge painting altogether.
5. He became a toll collector.

B. You can make a story out of the following sentences if you arrange them in an order that makes sense. First decide what the order should be. Then write the sentences as a paragraph. Be sure to indent the first word in the paragraph.

1. Laura explained that the alarm clock was set for seven.
2. Her teacher asked her why she was late.
3. Her teacher didn't understand why that made her late.
4. One day Laura arrived late for class.
5. Laura said it was because there were eight people in her family.

4. When to Begin a New Paragraph

Most of the stories that you write tell about several things happening. When you tell about several things, begin a new paragraph each time you tell about something new.

Here is an example of a story that has three paragraphs..

A Flying Cow

Donna was looking out her window one day. Suddenly she saw a cow fly over her house. She couldn't believe her eyes!

She ran to tell her mother and father about the flying cow. They just laughed. They thought she was teasing them. But she insisted it was true!

They all went outside together and looked up at the sky. There they saw a large, cow-shaped balloon. It was advertising a new hamburger restaurant.

Points to Observe

⊙ The first paragraph tells what Donna thought she saw from the window.

⊙ The second paragraph tells what happened when she told her parents what she saw.

288 ⊙ The third paragraph tells what Donna really saw.

For Practice

A. It isn't always easy to decide when to begin a new paragraph. And sometimes people disagree. Some people would say, for example, that the following story has two parts. They would divide it into two paragraphs. Other people would say it has three parts. They would divide it into three paragraphs.

What do you think? Would you divide this story into two paragraphs or three? What do other people in your class think?

Out for a Walk

One day I couldn't find my dog, Flip. I looked in my house and in my yard. I called and called, but he just wasn't around. I asked some of my friends to help me find Flip. Five of us went around looking in stores and backyards. Flip was nowhere to be found. When it was time for his supper, he came strolling in. He acted as though he'd just been out for a little walk. I never did find out where he had spent the afternoon.

B. Look at one of your own stories. Count how many paragraphs it has. Then read the story. Try to decide how many parts it has and where each part begins. See if you would still use the same number of paragraphs if you were writing the story today.

5. When to Use Capital Letters

⊙ Begin each sentence you write with a capital letter.

Put the hamburgers on the grill to cook.

⊙ Use a capital letter when you write the word *I*.

Did **I** say that?

⊙ Use capital letters when you write special names like these.

PERSONS:	**M**r. **R**oger **D**avis	STATES:	**N**orth **D**akota
STREETS:	**M**ain **S**treet	DAYS:	**W**ednesday
SCHOOLS:	**L**incoln **S**chool	MONTHS:	**J**uly
CITIES:	**L**os **A**ngeles	SPECIAL DAYS:	**T**hanksgiving

For Practice

A. Write these sentences. Be sure to begin each one with a capital letter. Also be sure that you use a capital when you write the word *I*.

1. Ann said that I should help you.

2. Where did I leave my bicycle?

B. Write these sentences. Be sure that you use capital letters when you write each special name in italics.

1. Is *Mr. Hall* your uncle?

2. *Ann Malloy* lives on *Forest Avenue*.

3. I went to the *Turner School* last year.

4. We went to *Denver* on our vacation.

5. I used to live in *Louisiana*.

6. Next *Tuesday* is a holiday.

7. My birthday comes in *February*.

8. My favorite holiday is *Christmas*.

6. What End Punctuation to Use

⊙ Use a period at the end of a sentence that makes a statement.

The tacos are all ready to eat.

⊙ Use a period at the end of a sentence that tells someone to do something.

Put the cookies in the oven.

⊙ Use a question mark at the end of a question.

Did you see the baby giraffe at the zoo?

⊙ Use an exclamation point at the end of a sentence that expresses strong feeling.

What a cute puppy you have!

For Practice

Read each sentence below. Decide whether it should end with a period, a question mark, or an exclamation point. Then write each sentence.

1. I have a white rat named Pete
   My sister doesn't like my white rat at all
   John stood in the middle of the kitchen

2. Are you ready to put up the tent
   Where did you put the tent stakes
   Why did Larry want to see me

3. Put your bicycles in the garage
   Wash your hands before supper
   Please take the packages into the house

4. What a scare you just gave me
   Look out for the car
   How dark the clouds look now

7. When to Use Commas

⊙ Use commas to set off *yes* and *no* at the beginning of a sentence.

> **Yes,** I know what you mean.
> **No,** I didn't do it.

⊙ Use commas to set off the name of a person being spoken to.

> **Mary,** what happened?
> Where are you going, **Sue?**

⊙ Use commas to separate words and word groups that come one after the other in a series.

> **Mary, Ellen, and Janet** are in my class.
> I had **a hamburger, some French fries, and a coke.**

For Practice

Write these sentences. Use commas where they are needed.

1. Yes I did go to the library yesterday.
   No I didn't see Andy there.
   Yes I saw Alan leave early.
   No I don't know where he went.

2. Alice where did you hide my pencil?
   When did you have your hair cut Maria?
   Don what is the name of your pet?
   Why are you leaving early Ramos?

3. I went fishing with Peter Dave and Joe.
   My hobbies are swimming reading and coin collecting.
   I painted my bicycle red white and blue.
   I bought a notebook a pen and a ruler.

8. When to Use Apostrophes

⊙ Use apostrophes to show where letters have been left out of contractions.

he is → he's   does not → doesn't

⊙ Use an apostrophe and an *s* when you want to make a word like *boy* show ownership.

one boy's coat   one boy's lunch

⊙ Use an apostrophe after the *s* when you want to make a word like *boys* show ownership.

two boys' coats   two boys' lunches

For Practice

A. Write each sentence. Use a contraction in place of each pair of words in italics. Choose from the contractions in the box.

1. Peter *is not* home.
2. They *do not* like chocolate ice cream.
3. *I am* his brother.

> don't
> isn't
> I'm

B. Write each sentence. Add **'s** to each word in ( ) to make it show ownership.

1. Where is (John) belt?
2. Is that your (friend) coat?
3. Who ate my (brother) lunch?

C. Write the second sentence in each pair. Add an **'** to each word in ( ) to make it show ownership.

1. I have four cousins. Those are my (cousins) bicycles.
2. I saw two girls. Those are the (girls) books.
3. I have three sisters. Those are my (sisters) coats.

9. How to Make Changes

When you are writing a story, you sometimes find that you need to make changes. If you are writing with pencil, you can erase. If you are using ink, though, it is hard to erase.

Below are some suggestions for making changes when you use ink.

⊙ Change small letters to capital letters this way.

Tom and I went swimming with ͣAlan.

⊙ Add a word or word group to a sentence this way.

David answered ^the telephone.

⊙ Cross out a word or word group this way.

The squirrel ~~he~~ took a nut from my hand.

⊙ Change a misspelled word this way.

Is Doris a ~~frend~~ friend of yours?

294

For Practice

A. Each sentence below needs to be changed. Copy the sentences just as they are, using ink. Then find the mistakes and make the needed changes.

1. In this sentence the word *Ann* needs a capital letter.

What did you tell ann?

2. In this sentence the word *when* is missing after *raining*.

It was raining we reached the lake.

3. This sentence has an extra word that needs crossing out.

We waited for in the storm shelter.

4. In this sentence the word *really* is misspelled.

We realy had to wait a long time.

B. Each sentence in the following story has a mistake in it. See if you can find each mistake. Then copy the story just as it is. Use ink. When you finish, make the needed changes in the story.

Oscar and the Clocks

Oscar was a man had trouble understanding things. One day his frend came to his house. oscar was throwing clocks out the window. His frend asked why Oscar would want to do that. Oscar said that he that he wanted to see time fly.

For Individual Needs

Usage

1. Choosing Between *I* and *Me*

Sentences with I

1. **Jim** talked to Ann.
2. **I** talked to Ann. } ⟹ 3. **Jim and I** talked to Ann.

Sentences with Me

4. Ann talked to **Jim.**
5. Ann talked to **me.** } ⟹ 6. Ann talked to **Jim and me.**

Points to Observe

⊙ Sentence *1* begins with *Jim,* and sentence *2* begins with *I.* Therefore, sentence *3* begins with *Jim and I.*

⊙ Sentence *4* ends with *Jim.* Sentence *5* ends with *me.* Therefore, sentence *6* ends with *Jim and me.*

For Practice

A. Read these sentences aloud for practice in using *I* and *me.*

1. *I* cooked dinner. *David and I* cooked dinner.
Debra ate with *me.* Debra ate with *David and me.*

2. *I* saw you on television. *Dora and I* saw you on television.
Carol saw *me.* Carol saw *Dora and me.*

3. *I* have a new fishing rod. *Ed and I* have new fishing rods.
Joe went fishing with *me.* Joe went fishing with *Ed and me.*

B. Write the second sentence in each pair. Complete it with *I* or *me.*

1. *I* baked a cake.
Louise and — baked a cake.

2. Joyce invited *me* to the party.
Joyce invited Ruby and — to the party.

3. Yvonne went to the zoo with *me.*
298   Yvonne went to the zoo with Clare and —.

2. Choosing Between *She* and *Her*

> **Sentences with She**
> 1. **Harriet** is here. ⎫
> 2. **She** is here.   ⎬ ⇒ 3. **Harriet and she** are here.
>
> **Sentences with Her**
> 4. Did you see **Harriet**? ⎫
> 5. Did you see **her**?   ⎬ ⇒ 6. Did you see **Harriet and her**?

Points to Observe

- ⊙ Sentence *1* begins with *Harriet*. Sentence *2* begins with *she*. Therefore, sentence *3* begins with *Harriet and she*.
- ⊙ Sentence *4* ends with *Harriet*. Sentence *5* ends with *her*. Therefore, sentence *6* ends with *Harriet and her*.

For Practice

A. Read these sentences aloud for practice in using *she* and *her*.

1. *She* went ice-skating. *She and Maria* went ice-skating.
   I saw *her*. I saw *her and Maria*.
2. *She* had a piece of pie. *She and Don* had some pie.
   I gave *her* some milk. I gave *her and Don* some milk.
3. *She* baked some cookies. *She and Betsy* baked some cookies.
   I helped *her*. I helped *Betsy and her*.

B. Write the second sentence in each pair. Complete it with *she* or *her*.

1. *She* takes piano lessons.
   — and Ruth take piano lessons.
2. I bought *her* some candy.
   I bought Margaret and — some candy.
3. I was talking to *her*.
   I was talking to Cynthia and —.

299

3. Choosing Between *He* and *Him*

Sentences with He
1. **Larry** saw Carl.
2. **He** saw Carl.
} ⟹ 3. **Larry and he** saw Carl.

Sentences with Him
4. Rita saw **Larry.**
5. Rita saw **him.**
} ⟹ 6. Rita saw **Larry and him.**

Points to Observe

⊙ Sentence *1* begins with *Larry*. Sentence *2* begins with *he*. Therefore, sentence *3* begins with *Larry and he*.

⊙ Sentence *4* ends with *Larry*, and sentence *5* ends with *him*. Therefore, sentence *6* ends with *Larry and him*.

For Practice

A. Read these sentences aloud for practice in using *he* and *him*.

1. *He* has a new bicycle. *He and Gail* have new bicycles.
   I went riding with *him*. I went riding with *Gail and him*.
2. *He* built a treehouse. *He and Willie* built a treehouse.
   I gave *him* a saw. I gave *Willie and him* a saw.
3. *He* broke a window. *He and Nathan* broke a window.
   I asked *him* to fix it. I asked *Nathan and him* to fix it.

B. Write these sentences. Complete each one with *he* or *him*.

1. — is playing baseball.
   — and Stanley are playing baseball.
2. Mr. Davis introduced — to us.
   Mr. Davis introduced Gloria and — to us.
3. I gave the pictures to —.
   I gave the pictures to Lois and —.

4. Choosing Between *We* and *Us*

Sentences with We

1. **Sara** is leaving now.
2. **We** are leaving now. $\Rightarrow$ 3. **Sara and we** are leaving now.

Sentences with Us

4. Mr. Yost paid **Sara.**
5. Mr. Yost paid **us.** $\Rightarrow$ 6. Mr. Yost paid **Sara and us.**

Points to Observe

⊙ Sentence *1* begins with *Sara*. Sentence *2* begins with *we*. Therefore, sentence *3* begins with *Sara and we*.

⊙ Sentence *4* ends with *Sara*, and sentence *5* ends with *us*. Therefore, sentence *6* ends with *Sara and us*.

For Practice

A. Practice reading these sentences aloud.

1. *We* swam across the lake. *Bill and we* swam across the lake. Beth swam with *us*. Beth swam with *Bill and us*.
2. *We* were hungry. *Lena and we* were hungry. Mother gave *us* lunch. Mother gave *Lena and us* lunch.
3. *We* played tennis. *Erika and we* played tennis. Mr. Rowe showed *us* how. Mr. Rowe showed *Erika and us* how.

B. Write these sentences. Complete each one with *we* or *us*.

1. — went to the movies.
   Artis and — went to the movies.
2. Frank helped — wash the dog.
   Frank helped Marc and — wash the dog.
3. Wait here with —.
   Wait here with Carrie and —.

301

5. Choosing Between *They* and *Them*

Points to Observe

⊙ Sentence *1* begins with *Al.* Sentence *2* begins with *they.* Therefore, sentence *3* begins with *Al and they.*

⊙ Sentence *4* ends with *Al,* and sentence *5* ends with *them.* Therefore, sentence *6* ends with *Al and them.*

For Practice

A. Practice reading these sentences aloud.

1. *They* explored the cave. *Ann and they* explored the cave. Henry went with *them.* Henry went with *Ann and them.*
2. *They* like hard candy. *Kathy and they* like hard candy. I bought some for *them.* I bought some for *Kathy and them.*
3. *They* sang a song. *Ella and they* sang a song. Tommy sang with *them.* Tommy sang with *Ella and them.*

B. Write the second sentence in each pair. Complete it with *they* or *them.*

1. *They* are ready to go to school now. Howard and — are ready to go to school now.
2. I saw *them* at the library. I saw George and — at the library.
3. Who is that talking to *them?* Who is that talking to Tom and —?

6. Choosing Between *Those* and *Them*

> 1. Hand **those books** to me, please.
> 2. Hand **those** to me.
> 3. Hand **them** to me.

Points to Observe

⊙ *Those* can be used before a noun like *books*, as in sentence *1*. It can also be used without a noun, as in sentence *2*.

⊙ *Them* is always used without a noun, as in sentence *3*.

For Practice

A. Read these sentences aloud. Notice how *those* and *them* are used.

1. I made *those sandwiches* myself. I made *those* myself. I made *them* myself.

2. Where did you buy *those shoes?* Where did you buy *those?* When did you buy *them?*

3. Who left *those toys* on the floor? Who left *those* on the floor? Who left *them* on the floor?

4. Where did you catch *those fish?* Where did you catch *those?* Where did you catch *them?*

5. Who put *those books* here? Who put *those* here? Who put *them* here?

B. Use the following word groups in sentences of your own.

1. those turtles	**4.** those lemons	**7.** those skates
2. those cars	**5.** those jets	**8.** those windows
3. those bottles	**6.** those cars	**9.** those dishes

7. Choosing Between *A* and *An*

$$\text{a} \begin{cases} \text{cherry} \\ \text{pear} \\ \text{lemon} \\ \text{banana} \\ \text{grape} \end{cases} \qquad \text{an} \begin{cases} \text{apple} \\ \text{egg} \\ \text{igloo} \\ \text{ostrich} \\ \text{umbrella} \end{cases}$$

Points to Observe

⊙ *A* is used before a word that begins with a consonant sound.
⊙ *An* is used before a word that begins with a vowel sound.

For Practice

A. Practice reading these sentences aloud.

1. I have *a* scratch.
I have *an* itch.

2. We saw *a* tiger.
We saw *an* elephant.

3. Mother peeled *a* potato.
Mother peeled *an* onion.

4. I had *a* raincoat.
I had *an* umbrella.

5. I made *a* snowball.
I found *an* icicle.

6. He wore *a* jacket.
He wore *an* overcoat.

7. John built *a* sailboat.
John built *an* iceboat.

8. Ann ate *a* plum.
Ann ate *an* orange.

9. Peter has *a* hatchet.
Peter has *an* ax.

10. I ate *a* pickle.
I ate *an* olive.

B. Use the following word groups in sentences. Write the sentences.

1. a mouse
2. an eagle
3. a garage

4. an uncle
5. a bell
6. an acorn

7. a lamp
8. an iceberg
9. a porcupine

8. Choosing Between *Isn't* and *Aren't*

Isn't	Aren't
She **isn't** ready.	We **aren't** ready.
He **isn't** ready.	You **aren't** ready.
It **isn't** ready.	They **aren't** ready.

Points to Observe

⊙ *Isn't* is used with *she, he,* and *it.*

⊙ *Aren't* is used with *we, you,* and *they.*

For Practice

A. Practice reading these pairs of sentences aloud. Listen for *isn't* and *aren't.*

1. She *isn't* coming.
They *aren't* coming.

2. He *isn't* here yet.
They *aren't* here yet.

3. It *isn't* important.
They *aren't* important.

4. She *isn't* in our class.
They *aren't* in our class.

5. It *isn't* hurt badly.
They *aren't* hurt badly.

6. He *isn't* going.
You *aren't* going.

7. He *isn't* lazy.
You *aren't* lazy.

8. She *isn't* sleepy.
We *aren't* sleepy.

9. She *isn't* late.
We *aren't* late.

10. He *isn't* hungry.
We *aren't* hungry.

B. Complete each sentence with *isn't* or *aren't.* Write each sentence.

1. It — far from here.
2. You — as tall as my brother.
3. The football game — over yet.
4. They — the ones that I wanted.
5. We — going to be on time, I'm afraid.

305

9. Choosing Between *Was* and *Were*

Was	Were
I **was** hungry.	We **were** hungry.
She **was** giggling.	You **were** giggling.
He **was** sorry.	They **were** sorry.
It **was** broken.	

Points to Observe

- ⊙ *Was* is used with *I, she, he,* and *it.*
- ⊙ *Were* is used with *we, you,* and *they.*

For Practice

A. Practice reading these sentences aloud. Listen for *was* and *were.*

1. I *was* tired.
   We *were* tired.
2. He *was* absent.
   They *were* absent.
3. She *was* upset.
   They *were* upset.
4. I *was* trying to help.
   We *were* trying to help.

5. He *was* late today.
   They *were* late today.
6. She *was* picking flowers.
   They *were* picking flowers.
7. That joke *was* funny.
   They *were* funny.
8. She *was* reading.
   You *were* reading.

B. Turn each statement into a question beginning with *were.* Write each question.

1. You were going to tell me something.
2. They were going to help you paint.
3. We were supposed to read that story.
4. They were playing in the park.
5. You were on the wrong bus.

10. Choosing Between *Wasn't* and *Weren't*

Wasn't	Weren't
I **wasn't** there.	We **weren't** there.
He **wasn't** there.	You **weren't** there.
She **wasn't** there.	They **weren't** there.
It **wasn't** there.	

Points to Observe

⊙ *Wasn't* is used with *I, he, she,* and *it.*

⊙ *Weren't* is used with *we, you,* and *they.*

For Practice

A. Practice reading these sentences aloud.

1. I *wasn't* finished.
   We *weren't* finished.

2. He *wasn't* sick.
   They *weren't* sick.

3. She *wasn't* at home.
   You *weren't* at home.

4. It *wasn't* my pet.
   They *weren't* my pets.

5. I *wasn't* surprised.
   We *weren't* surprised.

6. He *wasn't* friendly.
   They *weren't* friendly.

7. She *wasn't* waiting.
   They *weren't* waiting.

8. It *wasn't* my pencil.
   Those *weren't* my pencils.

9. I *wasn't* worried.
   We *weren't* worried.

10. I *wasn't* the winner.
    You *weren't* the winner.

B. Complete each sentence with *wasn't* or *weren't*. Write each sentence.

1. I — the one you saw.
2. We — anywhere near the airport.
3. He — going to go to the city.
4. They — supposed to tell you the secret.
5. You — supposed to do that.

11. Choosing Between *Doesn't* and *Don't*

Doesn't	Don't
My brother **doesn't** like pizza.	My brothers **don't** like pizza.
He **doesn't** like pizza.	They **don't** like pizza.

Points to Observe

⊙ *Doesn't* is used with words that mean only one person or thing, like *my brother* or *he*.

⊙ *Don't* is used with words that mean several persons or things, like *my brothers* or *they*.

For Practice

A. Practice reading these sentences aloud.

1. The boy *doesn't* know me.
   The boys *don't* know me.

2. Mary *doesn't* want any.
   The girls *don't* want any.

3. He *doesn't* speak French.
   They *don't* speak French.

4. She *doesn't* understand.
   They *don't* understand.

5. He *doesn't* swim at all.
   They *don't* swim at all.

6. John *doesn't* care.
   They *don't* care.

7. It *doesn't* look good.
   They *don't* look good.

8. The dog *doesn't* bark.
   The dogs *don't* bark.

9. It *doesn't* work.
   They *don't* work.

10. Anita *doesn't* see it.
    They *don't* see it.

B. Turn each statement into a question that begins with *doesn't*. Write each question.

1. The highway doesn't end here.
2. Andrew doesn't know the answer.
3. The show doesn't start until noon.
4. He doesn't believe me.
5. Jerry doesn't know how to swim.

12. Choosing Between *Saw* and *Seen*, *Ate* and *Eaten*

Saw, Seen	Ate, Eaten
I **saw** Tom.	He **ate** bread.
I **have seen** Tom.	He **has eaten** bread.
I **had seen** Tom.	He **had eaten** bread.

Points to Observe

⊙ *Saw* is used alone. *Seen* is used with *have*, *has*, or *had*.

⊙ *Ate* is used alone. *Eaten* is used with *have*, *has*, or *had*.

For Practice

A. Read these sentences aloud until they sound right to you.

Saw, Seen	Ate, Eaten
1. We *saw* the game. We *have seen* the game. We *had seen* the game.	**1.** The boys *ate* lunch. The boys *have eaten* lunch. The boys *had eaten* lunch.
2. He *saw* my friend. He *has seen* my friend. He *had seen* my friend.	**2.** My dog *ate* the steak. My dog *has eaten* the steak. My dog *had eaten* the steak.
3. Sheila *saw* Sara. Sheila *has seen* Sara. Sheila *had seen* Sara.	**3.** I *ate* an avocado. I *have eaten* an avocado. I *had eaten* an avocado.
4. They *saw* the movie. They *have seen* the movie. They *had seen* the movie.	**4.** The bird *ate* the worm. The bird *has eaten* the worm. The bird *had eaten* the worm.

B. Write eight sentences. Use the following words.

1. saw

2. have seen

3. has seen

4. had seen

5. ate

6. have eaten

7. has eaten

8. had eaten

13. Choosing Between *Ran* and *Run,* *Came* and *Come*

Ran, Run	Came, Come
Leroy **ran** a mile.	Linda **came** too late.
Leroy **has run** a mile.	Linda **has come** too late.
Leroy **had run** a mile.	Linda **had come** too late.

Points to Observe

⊙ *Ran* is used alone. *Run* is used with *have, has,* or *had.*

⊙ *Came* is used alone. *Come* is used with *have, has,* or *had.*

For Practice

A. Read the following sentences aloud until the words in italics sound right to you.

Ran, Run

1. He *ran* upstairs.
   He *has run* upstairs.
   He *had run* upstairs.
2. I *ran* out of money.
   I *have run* out of money.
   I *had run* out of money.
3. It *ran* out of gas.
   It *has run* out of gas.
   It *had run* out of gas.

Came, Come

1. We *came* prepared.
   We *have come* prepared.
   We *had come* prepared.
2. She *came* with presents.
   She *has come* with presents.
   She *had come* with presents.
3. I *came* to help.
   I *have come* to help.
   I *had come* to help.

B. Complete each sentence below with *ran* or *run, came* or *come.* Write each sentence.

Ran, Run

1. Ken — down the street.
2. He has — on this track.
3. The horses have — away.
4. The motor had — down.

Came, Come

1. Frank — home.
2. The birds have — home.
3. He has — with Walter.
4. They had — to a stop.

14. Choosing Between *Did* and *Done, Went* and *Gone*

Did, Done	Went, Gone
I **did** the job.	Sue **went** home.
I **have done** the job.	Sue **has gone** home.
I **had done** the job.	Sue **had gone** home.

Points to Observe

⊙ *Did* is used alone. *Done* is used with *have, has,* or *had.*

⊙ *Went* is used alone. *Gone* is used with *have, has,* or *had.*

For Practice

A. Read the following sentences aloud until the words in italics sound right to you.

Did, Done

1. We *did* the dishes.
   We *have done* the dishes.
   We *had done* the dishes.
2. Jane *did* a dance.
   Jane *has done* a dance.
   Jane *had done* a dance.
3. I *did* my homework.
   I *have done* my homework.
   I *had done* my homework.

Went, Gone

1. He *went* away.
   He *has gone* away.
   He *had gone* away.
2. We *went* often.
   We *have gone* often.
   We *had gone* often.
3. Shirley *went* alone.
   Shirley *has gone* alone.
   Shirley *had gone* alone.

B. Complete each sentence below with *did* or *done, went* or *gone.* Write each sentence.

Did, Done

1. She — it already.
2. I have — it already.
3. Sid has — it already.
4. We had — it already.

Went, Gone

1. Father — to work.
2. I have — to work.
3. Tom has — to work.
4. They had — to work.

15. Choosing Between *Gave* and *Given, Took* and *Taken*

Gave, Given	Took, Taken
I **gave** him money.	Eric **took** a train.
I **have given** him money.	Eric **has taken** a train.
I **had given** him money.	Eric **had taken** a train.

Points to Observe

⊙ *Gave* is used alone. *Given* is used with *have, has,* or *had.*

⊙ *Took* is used alone. *Taken* is used with *have, has,* or *had.*

For Practice

A. Read the following sentences aloud until the words in italics sound right to you.

Gave, Given

1. We *gave* a play.
   We *have given* a play.
   We *had given* a play.
2. She *gave us* candy.
   She *has given* us candy.
   She *had given* us candy.
3. They *gave* a party.
   They *have given* a party.
   They *had given* a party.

Took, Taken

1. It *took* too long.
   It *has taken* too long.
   It *had taken* too long.
2. We *took* a trip.
   We *have taken* a trip.
   We *had taken* a trip.
3. John *took* his time.
   John *has taken* his time.
   John *had taken* his time.

B. Complete the following sentences. Use *gave* or *given, took* or *taken*. Write the sentences.

Gave, Given

1. You — me a gift.
2. You have — me a gift.
3. She has — me a gift.
4. I had — you a gift.

Took, Taken

1. Bob — his time.
2. You have — your time.
3. Jim has — his time.
4. I had — my time.

16. Choosing Between *Knew* and *Known*, *Threw* and *Thrown*

Knew, Known	Threw, Thrown
You **knew** the answer.	He **threw** the ball.
You **have known** the answer.	He **has thrown** the ball.
You **had known** the answer.	He **had thrown** the ball.

Points to Observe

○ *Knew* is used alone. *Known* is used with *have, has,* or *had.*

○ *Threw* is used alone. *Thrown* is used with *have, has,* or *had.*

For Practice

A. Read the following sentences aloud until the words in italics sound right to you.

Knew, Known	Threw, Thrown
1. He *knew* my brother. He *has known* my brother. He *had known* my brother.	**1.** I *threw* the keys away. I *have thrown* the keys away. I *had thrown* the keys away.
2. We *knew* her well. We *have known* her well. We *had known* her well.	**2.** Len *threw* the football. Len *has thrown* the football. Len *had thrown* the football.
3. Carl *knew* the answer. Carl *has known* the answer. Carl *had known* the answer.	**3.** I *threw* the ball. I *have thrown* the ball. I *had thrown* the ball.

B. Complete the sentences below. Use *knew* or *known, threw* or *thrown.*

Knew, Known	Threw, Thrown
1. I — him.	**1.** She — it away.
2. I have — him.	**2.** You have — it away.
3. She has — him.	**3.** She has — it away.
4. You had — him.	**4.** We had — it away.

313

17. Choosing Between *Drove* and *Driven*, *Wrote* and *Written*

Drove, Driven	Wrote, Written
I **drove** the truck.	He **wrote** a letter.
I have **driven** the truck.	He **has written** a letter.
I had **driven** the truck.	He **had written** a letter.

Points to Observe

⊙ *Drove* is used alone. *Driven* is used with *have*, *has*, or *had*.

⊙ *Wrote* is used alone. *Written* is used with *have*, *has*, or *had*.

For Practice

A. Read the following sentences aloud until they sound right to you.

Drove, Driven

1. He *drove* all day.
   He *has driven* all day.
   He *had driven* all day.
2. You *drove* the car.
   You *have driven* the car.
   You *had driven* the car.
3. She *drove* the jeep.
   She *has driven* the jeep.
   She *had driven* the jeep.

Wrote, Written

1. I *wrote* a long letter.
   I *have written* a long letter.
   I *had written* a long letter.
2. Sally *wrote* a poem.
   Sally *has written* a poem.
   Sally *had written* a poem.
3. We *wrote* term papers.
   We *have written* term papers.
   We *had written* term papers.

B. Complete the sentences below. Use *drove* or *driven*, *wrote* or *written*.

Drove, Driven

1. Father — slowly.
2. I have — slowly.
3. Father has — slowly.
4. I had — slowly.

Wrote, Written

1. I — a note.
2. I have — a note.
3. She has — a note.
4. I had — a note.

18. Choosing Between *Rode* and *Ridden*, *Fell* and *Fallen*

Rode, Ridden	Fell, Fallen
I **rode** Ann's bike.	Jim fell down.
I **have ridden** Ann's bike.	Jim **has fallen** down.
I **had ridden** Ann's bike.	Jim **had fallen** down.

Points to Observe

○ *Rode* is used alone. *Ridden* is used with *have*, *has*, or *had*.

○ *Fell* is used alone. *Fallen* is used with *have*, *has*, or *had*.

For Practice

A. Read the following sentences aloud until the words in italics sound right to you.

Rode, Ridden

1. We *rode* all night.
   We *have ridden* all night.
   We *had ridden* all night.
2. She *rode* by the house.
   She *has ridden* by the house.
   She *had ridden* by the house.
3. I *rode* Jay's horse.
   I *have ridden* Jay's horse.
   I *had ridden* Jay's horse.

Fell, Fallen

1. The snow *fell* all day.
   The snow *has fallen* all day.
   The snow *had fallen* all day.
2. Rocks *fell* from above.
   Rocks *have fallen* from above.
   Rocks *had fallen* from above.
3. They *fell* overboard.
   They *have fallen* overboard.
   They *had fallen* overboard.

B. Complete the sentences below with *rode* or *ridden*, *fell* or *fallen*. Write each sentence.

Rode, Ridden

1. I — in a canoe.
2. You have — in a canoe.
3. Rita has — in a canoe.
4. They had — in a canoe.

Fell, Fallen

1. Jan — on the ice.
2. I have — on the ice.
3. Tom has — on the ice.
4. We had — on the ice.

For Individual Needs

More Practice

Pages 16–17   Word Order in Sentences

Put each group of words below in sentence order. Write the sentences that you make.

1. game a played new we
2. sounds story your exciting
3. the flag the folded girls
4. package Stan a mailed
5. my changed mind I

6. Lisa deer the fed
7. butcher the cut meat the
8. camera our borrowed Kara
9. Chris piano the play can
10. left is sandwich one

Pages 18–19   Changing the Meaning

Change the meaning of each sentence below by changing the word order. Write the new sentences.

1. Jean thanked the speaker.
2. Her smile changed to a frown.
3. Max watched Bev skate.
4. Nancy waited for her cousin.
5. A truck parked behind the car.

6. Paul loaned Peggy a dime.
7. The tent is in the box.
8. Janet told Greg a joke.
9. The clowns followed the band.
10. Ken asked Val a question.

Page 20   Writing Names

Write the following sentences. Use capital letters where they belong.

1. Paula miles walked two miles.
2. My friend robin saw a robin.
3. Marlene joy jumped for joy.
4. Give violet the violet crayon.
5. Paul drew drew a map for us.

6. Ed rover named his dog rover.
7. Pat hall stood in the hall.
8. Sandra's cat is named cat.
9. Tim fry will fry the bacon.
10. The mark was made by mark rix.   317

Page 21   Writing <u>Mr.</u>, <u>Mrs.</u>, and <u>Miss</u>

Write the following names. Use capital letters and periods where they belong.

1. miss julie barrett

2. mr bruce childs

3. mr edward fontana

4. miss claire goldstein

5. mr anthony ivanic

6. miss katherine kraus

7. mr ralph lippman

8. mrs emily nolan

9. mr philip rizzo

10. mrs karen unger

Pages 42–43   Statements

Seven of the following sentences are statements. Write them on your paper.

1. The mirror was cracked.

2. The soup was hot.

3. Where is the cave?

4. Carmen won the contest.

5. The knife is sharp.

6. Was the movie good?

7. This puzzle is easy.

8. My sister is a pilot.

9. How tall are you?

10. The store was crowded.

Pages 44–45   One Kind of Question

Change each statement into a *yes/no* question by changing the order of the words. Write the questions.

1. The blanket is warm.

2. The gifts are wrapped.

3. The keys are on the table.

4. Cindy is playing tennis.

5. The motor is running.

6. The door was left open.

7. The suitcases were packed.

8. You are going on your vacation.

9. Her brother was sleepy.

10. The visitors were leaving.

Pages 46–47   Yes/No Questions with <u>Do</u> and <u>Did</u>

Change each statement into a *yes/no* question beginning with *do* or *did*. Write the questions.

1. The conductor took the ticket.
2. Her eyes sparkle.
3. The fur felt soft.
4. Roosters crow in the morning.
5. The flowers looked fresh.
6. Rafts float on water.
7. You collect stamps.
8. The ice cream melted.
9. Turtles have shells.
10. A man answered the phone.

Page 48   Names of Streets and Schools

Write the name of each street and school below. Use capital letters where they belong.

Streets

1. spencer lane
2. surry street
3. oakley avenue
4. willow lane

Schools

1. frankton high school
2. cunningham school
3. malcolm middle school
4. arlington high school

Page 49   Names of Cities and States

Write the sentences below. Use capital letters for the names of all cities and states.

1. The ranch is near waco, texas.
2. Her aunt lives in akron, ohio.
3. We camped near salem, oregon.
4. It was 103° in yuma, arizona.
5. Call us from atlanta, georgia.
6. They moved to boise, idaho.
7. The gold is from nome, alaska.
8. The map shows hilo, hawaii.

319

Pages 70–71   Two Kinds of Questions

A. Change each *yes/no* question into a *wh*-question beginning with *when*. Write each *wh*-question.

1. Did you play softball?

2. Did Al ride the subway?

3. Will we meet the reporter?

4. Did you learn to skate?

5. Did the package arrive?

6. Does Sue deliver papers?

B. Change each *yes/no* question into a *wh*-question beginning with *where*. Write each *wh*-question.

1. Did the campers build a fire?

2. Will you hang the picture?

3. Did you eat lunch?

4. Did she leave her umbrella?

5. Did Miss Linsay park the car?

6. Did you go swimming?

Pages 72–73   Questions Beginning with <u>Who</u> or <u>How</u>

A. Change each statement into a *wh*-question beginning with *who*. Write each *wh*-question.

1. Nelda gave a report.

2. Doug used the telephone.

3. Sara hit a home run.

4. No one heard the alarm.

5. The cook prepared dinner.

6. We made the costumes.

B. Change each *yes/no* question into a *wh*-question beginning with *how*. Write each *wh*-question.

1. Did Leslie help you?

2. Did your canary escape?

3. Do the captains decide?

4. Did Teresa unlock the drawer?

5. Do spiders spin webs?

6. Does the jacket fit?

Page 74   Writing the Names of Days and Months

Write each sentence below. Use capital letters for the names of all days and months.

1. The club meets every monday.

2. I take lessons on saturday.

3. They took a trip last august.

4. The big game is friday night.

5. Her birthday is in october.

6. The show begins next thursday.

7. We went sledding in january.

8. The park opens again in may.

9. Dad buys groceries on tuesday.

10. They plan to move in march.

Page 75   Writing Names of Special Days

Write each sentence below. Use capital letters for all names of special days.

1. The beach closed on labor day.

2. Visit us on thanksgiving day.

3. Wear a costume on halloween.

4. When is child health day?

5. The race is on memorial day.

6. We got up early on easter.

7. They voted on election day.

8. I called home on mother's day.

9. I planted a tree on arbor day.

10. Give candy on valentine's day.

Pages 96–97   The Two Parts of a Sentence

Make up sentences by adding subjects and predicates to the following sentence parts. Write each sentence that you make.

Add Subjects

1. — roared loudly.

2. — searched for a clue.

3. — decided to leave.

4. — struggled to get loose.

5. — loaded the furniture.

Add Predicates

1. Our neighbor —.

2. The curious kitten —.

3. A loud cry —.

4. Kangaroos —.

5. A giant shadow —.

321

Pages 98–99   Adding Predicates

Make up sentences by adding two different predicates to each subject below. Write each sentence that you make.

1. Our new library —.
2. The top shelf —.
3. A special program —.
4. The busy beavers —.
5. A large pumpkin —.

6. A bright flame —.
7. The large snowflakes —.
8. A thunderstorm —.
9. The young calf —.
10. The shiny buttons —.

Pages 100–101   Adding Subjects

Make up sentences by adding two different subjects to each predicate below. Write each sentence that you make.

1. — guarded the entrance.
2. — surprised us.
3. — is knocking at the door.
4. — swallowed a fly.
5. — took our tickets.

6. — flashes off and on.
7. — scattered the papers.
8. — are directing traffic.
9. — jingled in his pocket.
10. — makes me happy.

Page 103   Capital Letters in Story Titles

Write each story title below. Use capital letters where they are needed.

1. three for the circus
2. airplane adventure
3. stuck in the snow
4. screams in the night
5. journey to the moon

6. camping in the mountains
7. monkeys on vacation
8. doughnuts by the dozen
9. plenty of surprises
10. searching for buried treasure

Pages 126–127　Nouns

Decide which of the following words can be used as nouns. Use the test sentence below to help you. Then write the nouns.

1. pencil
2. barrel
3. lively
4. butterfly
5. huge

6. balloon
7. handle
8. listen
9. shelf
10. necklace

Test Sentence

Do you see the —?

Pages 128–129　Some Forms of Nouns

Write each sentence below. Use the plural form of the noun in ( ).

1. The — tickled. (feather)
2. All the — were taken. (seat)
3. The — were late. (bus)
4. We hiked five —. (mile)
5. The — came off. (button)

6. The — were loaded. (base)
7. The — passed quickly. (hour)
8. Four — of snow fell. (inch)
9. The — were juicy. (orange)
10. We hid behind the —. (bush)

Pages 130–131　More Forms of Nouns

Write each sentence below. Use the plural form of the noun in ( ).

1. Four — wore hats. (woman)
2. We spotted three —. (deer)
3. The — do heavy work. (ox)
4. I saw several —. (goose)
5. Three — won prizes. (sheep)

6. She cleaned my —. (tooth)
7. The — played tag. (child)
8. He is six — tall. (foot)
9. Five — stood up. (man)
10. Two — scurried by. (mouse)

323

Pages 152–153   Noun Determiners

Write each sentence below. Underline the noun determiner in each sentence that you write.

1. Those ribbons are velvet.
2. Two pages are torn.
3. That mistake was corrected.
4. The jewels are missing.
5. This bread is homemade.

6. These branches are dangerous.
7. One slice filled me up.
8. A jet soared by.
9. Three letters came today.
10. An umbrella keeps you dry.

Pages 154–155   Nouns in the Subject Part

Add a subject part to each predicate given below. Use a determiner and a singular noun in each sentence. Write the sentences.

1. — fell from the tree.
2. — practiced after school.
3. — followed me home.
4. — is rusty.
5. — jumped out of the bushes.

6. — made us laugh.
7. — tastes too sweet.
8. — wins the prize.
9. — taught us a game.
10. — rode on an elephant.

Pages 156–157   Alphabetical Order

Write the words in each list in alphabetical order.

1	2	3	4
banana	lake	canoe	piano
watermelon	ocean	plane	violin
peach	stream	train	flute
coconut	brook	automobile	trumpet
grape	river	bicycle	banjo

Pages 158–159   More about Alphabetical Order

Decide which letter to look at to put each list in alphabetical order. Write the words in each list in alphabetical order.

1	2	3	4
airport	forest	peace	smile
arrow	friend	picnic	shadow
aunt	feather	program	sugar
answer	flame	package	shovel
alarm	family	potato	size

Pages 176–177   Words with Prefixes

Write the word in each pair below that contains a prefix.

1. uncover, cover
2. please, displease
3. arrange, rearrange
4. unpack, pack
5. pretest, test

6. display, play
7. count, recount
8. unfasten, fasten
9. preheat, heat
10. read, reread

Pages 178–179   Words with Suffixes

Write the word in each pair below that contains a suffix.

1. paint, painter
2. brightly, bright
3. helper, help
4. gray, grayish
5. pitch, pitcher

6. lovely, love
7. exact, exactly
8. clownish, clown
9. travel, traveler
10. sheepish, sheep

325

Pages 180–181   Proper Nouns

Write the example in each pair below that is a proper noun.

1. Friday, weekday
2. Mexico, country
3. street, Adams Street
4. Roseann Walker, girl
5. Pacific Ocean, ocean
6. Lake Louise, lake
7. park, Lincoln Park
8. Nile River, river
9. holiday, Labor Day
10. state, Texas

Pages 182–183   Proper Nouns in the Subject Part

Use a proper noun as the subject of each sentence below. Write the sentences. Use capital letters to begin the proper nouns.

1. — is a busy month.
2. — moved here last summer.
3. — rides the bus to school.
4. — is a beautiful city.
5. — is not far from here.
6. — is my favorite holiday.
7. — wrote me a letter.
8. — spoke to our class.
9. — is our team captain.
10. — is a place I want to visit.

Pages 204–205   Adding a Prefix and a Suffix

Write the word in each pair below that has both a prefix and a suffix.

1. uncomfortable, discomfort
2. refill, refillable
3. disgraceful, disgrace
4. uneven, unevenly
5. unreasonable, reasonable
6. disorder, disorderly
7. unlawful, lawful
8. renewable, renew
9. dishonor, dishonorable
10. fairness, unfairness

Pages 206–207   Adding Two Suffixes

Write the word in each pair below that ends with two suffixes.

1. fearlessly, unlikely
2. unfaithful, tearfully
3. cheerfully, unclearly
4. restlessness, unevenly
5. unselfish, selfishly

6. unsuccessful, successfully
7. hopelessly, distasteful
8. unthoughtful, thoughtfulness
9. needlessly, unhealthful
10. distrustful, lifelessness

Pages 208–209   Personal Pronouns

Write each sentence below. Underline the personal pronoun in each sentence that you write.

1. He wrote a poem.
2. The letter is from them.
3. She delivered the message.
4. I ate the whole pizza.
5. The class elected her.

6. Did you find the key?
7. We watched the soccer game.
8. They visited the museum.
9. The noise awoke us.
10. It stuck to my hand.

Pages 210–211   Personal Pronouns as the Subject Part

Complete each sentence below with a personal pronoun that can be used as a subject. Use at least five different personal pronouns in the sentences that you write.

1. — slid down the hill.
2. — chuckled at the cartoon.
3. — landed in the tree.
4. — is raking the leaves.
5. — am tired now.

6. — untied the knot.
7. — is stirring the batter.
8. — made loud noises.
9. — are planning the program.
10. — roasted marshmallows.

327

Write each sentence below. Underline the verb in each sentence that you write.

1. The barber trims my hair.
2. Kate poured a glass of milk.
3. We rested under a tree.
4. The fans cheered for the team.
5. Our meeting begins soon.
6. Terry whisked the crumbs away.
7. Papers scattered everywhere.
8. Sue played a drum solo.
9. My uncle owns a boat.
10. She skinned her knee.

A. The subject of each sentence below is singular. Write each sentence. Change each subject from singular to plural. Make the needed change in the verb.

1. The clown makes us laugh.
2. The sign points the way.
3. The tire needs air.
4. The runner looks tired.
5. The ship sails tomorrow.
6. The picture tells a story.
7. The glass breaks easily.
8. My sister skates well.
9. The towel feels damp.
10. The dancer moves gracefully.

B. The subject of each sentence below is plural. Write each sentence. Change each subject from plural to singular. Make the needed change in the verb.

1. The stores stay open late.
2. The dogs obey the trainer.
3. The hikers stop to rest.
4. The pies smell delicious.
5. The shades dim the light.
6. The books belong on the shelf.
7. The elephants perform tricks.
8. The cushions feel soft.
9. The players keep score.
10. The pickles taste sour.

Pages 240–241   Writing Contractions

Write each sentence below. Use a contraction to take the place of the words in italics in each sentence.

1. The bell *has not* rung yet.
2. They *do not* expect us.
3. These flowers *are not* real.
4. He *would not* wait in line.
5. Laura *did not* ride her bike.
6. We *should not* wander too far.
7. My parents *could not* come.
8. The note *had not* been signed.
9. The car *is not* in the garage.
10. I *have not* seen your scarf.

Pages 242–243   More about Writing Contractions

Write each sentence below. Use a contraction to take the place of the words in italics in each sentence.

1. *I am* almost finished.
2. *They will* meet us later.
3. *You are* a good friend.
4. *We have* run out of paint.
5. *He had* forgotten the time.
6. *She has* got lots of energy.
7. *It is* past ten o'clock.
8. *You have* watched enough TV.
9. *What is* the latest news?
10. *They are* visiting our class.

Pages 264–265   A Verb Form That Goes with <u>Yesterday</u>

Write each sentence below, changing *now* to *yesterday*. Be sure to change the form of the verb in each sentence.

1. The signals flash now.
2. The horses gallop now.
3. The class votes now.
4. My sister plays golf now.
5. They serve dinner now.
6. The actors perform now.
7. We change partners now.
8. The band practices now.
9. The stores close now.
10. The roof leaks now.

Pages 266–267   More Verb Forms

Write each of the sentences below, changing *now* to *yesterday*. Be sure to change the form of the verb in each sentence.

1. The canoe race begins now.
2. The pages tear easily now.
3. The club meets at noon now.
4. We take lunch money now.
5. Leaves fall gently now.

6. The whistle blows now.
7. The judges choose now.
8. Everyone rides the bus now.
9. My friend writes to me now.
10. The president speaks now.

Pages 268–269   Writing Words That Show Ownership

Write the following word groups. Make each word in ( ) show ownership by adding *'s*.

1. a (lion) cub
2. our (country) flag
3. (Ellen) scarf
4. one (player) uniform
5. the (passenger) ticket

6. the (woman) job
7. the (tree) branches
8. my (sister) hobby
9. the (car) engine
10. my (brother) radio

Pages 270–271   More about Words That Show Ownership

Write the following word groups. Make each word in ( ) show ownership by adding an apostrophe after the *s*.

1. the (nations) leaders
2. our (neighbors) yards
3. the (reporters) questions
4. the (shoppers) carts
5. my (friends) names

6. the (painters) brushes
7. the (twins) birthday
8. the (teams) captains
9. the (campers) tents
10. the (speakers) voices

Index

Proper nouns (*continued*)
   used as subjects, 182–183, 188, 189
Punctuation marks
   apostrophes, 240–241, 242–243, 244, 245, 268–269, 270–271, 272, 273, 293
   commas, 102, 104, 105, 292
   exclamation points, 291
   periods, 21, 22, 23, 42–43, 50, 51, 291
   question marks, 44–45, 46–47, 50, 51, 291

Questions
   punctuation of, 291
   wh-, 70–71, 72–73, 76, 77
   yes/no, 44–45, 46–47, 50, 51, 70–71, 72–73, 76, 77

Ran, run, 310
Rands, William Brighty, 60–61
Riddles, writing, 164–165, 192–193
Role-playing, 26–27, 28–29, 30–31, 80–81, 166–167, 194–195, 250–251

Saw, seen, 309
Sentences
   capital letters to begin, 290
   end punctuation of, 291
   main parts of, 96–97, 104, 105
   predicates of, 96–97, 98–99, 104, 105
   statements, 42–43, 50, 51
   subjects of, 96–97, 100–101, 104, 105, 154–155, 160, 161
   *wh-*questions, 70–71, 72–73, 76, 77

word order in, 16–17, 18–19, 22, 23, 44–45
yes/no questions, 44–45, 46–47, 50, 51, 70–71, 72–73, 76, 77
Seuss, Dr., 194
She, her, 299
Sounds
   and language, 14–15, 22
   letters for, 40–41, 50, 51
   and syllables, 92–93, 104, 105
   in words, 38–39
Statements
   defined, 42
   punctuation of, 42–43, 50, 51, 291
   word order in, 16–17, 18–19, 22, 23
   and *wh-*questions, 72–73, 76, 77
   and *yes/no* questions, 44–45, 46–47
Stories
   making up, for role-playing, 30–31, 80–81, 166–167, 194–195, 250–251
   telling, 52–53, 191
   writing, 56–57, 112–114, 136–138, 139–141
Story titles, writing, 103, 104, 105, 285
Stress, in words, 94–95, 104, 105
Subjects
   nouns in, 154–155, 160, 161
   pronouns in, 210–211, 216, 217
   proper nouns in, 182–183, 188, 189
   of sentences, 96–97, 104, 105
Suffixes
   building words with, 178–179, 204–205, 216, 217

334

(ACKNOWLEDGMENTS continued from page 4.)

permission. / "In Time of Silver Rain" by Langston Hughes: From FIELDS OF WONDER by Langston Hughes. Copyright, 1947, by Langston Hughes. Published, 1947, by Alfred A. Knopf, Inc. and reprinted with their permission. / "Fight" by Jean Jaszi: Reprinted from THE READING OF POETRY by William D. Sheldon, Nellie Lyons, and Polly Rouault. Published, 1963, by Allyn and Bacon. / "Sneeze" by Maxine Kumin: Reprinted by permission of G. P. Putnam's Sons from NO ONE WRITES A LETTER TO THE SNAIL by Maxine Kumin and illustrated by Bean Allen. Text copyright © 1962 by Maxine Kumin. / "The Balloon" from IN THE MIDDLE OF THE TREES by Karla Kuskin: Copyright © 1958 by Karla Kuskin. Reprinted by permission of Harper & Row, Publishers. / "The Little Turtle" by Vachel Lindsay: From COLLECTED POEMS by Vachel Lindsay, published by The Macmillan Company. Copyright © 1920 by The Macmillan Company, renewed, 1948, by Elizabeth C. Lindsay. / "Furry Bear" from the book NOW WE ARE SIX by A. A. Milne. Decorations by E. H. Shepard. Copyright 1927 by E. P. Dutton & Co., Inc. Renewal © 1955 by A. A. Milne. Published by E. P. Dutton & Co., Inc. and reprinted with permission. / "Missing" from the book WHEN WE WERE VERY YOUNG by A. A. Milne. Decorations by E. H. Shepard. Copyright 1924 by E. P. Dutton & Co., Inc. Renewal 1952 by A. A. Milne. Published by E. P. Dutton & Co., Inc. and reprinted with their permission. / "I Want to Go Traveling" by Ilo Orleans: Reprinted from I WATCH THE WORLD GO BY by Ilo Orleans. Published, 1961, by Henry Z. Walck, Inc. / "An Easy Decision" from COLLECTED POEMS by Kenneth Patchen: Copyright 1952 by Kenneth Patchen, © 1957 by New Directions Publishing Corporation. Reprinted by permission of New Directions Publishing Corporation. / "Godfrey Gordon Gustavus Gore" by William Brighty Rands: Reprinted from MY POETRY BOOK by Grace Thompson Huffard and Laura Mae Carlisle in collaboration with Helen Ferris. Copyright, 1934, 1956, by Holt, Rinehart and Winston, Inc. / Excerpt from ONE FISH, TWO FISH, RED FISH, BLUE FISH by Dr. Seuss: Copyright, 1960, by Dr. Seuss. Published by Beginner Books, a Division of Random House, Inc. and reprinted with their permission. / "Advice to Children" by Carolyn Wells: Reprinted from OH WHAT NONSENSE POEMS selected by William Cole. Text copyright, 1966, by William Cole. Published, 1966, by the Viking Press.